Ancient Secrets of the Bible

INVESTIGATING THE MYSTERIES OF SCRIPTURE

Time
HOME ENTERTAINMENT

AMERICAN BIBLE SOCIETY

Time Home Entertainment

Publisher
Jim Childs

Vice President, Business Development & Strategy
Steven Sandonato

Executive Director, Marketing Services
Carol Pittard

Executive Director, Retail & Special Sales
Tom Mifsud

Executive Publishing Director
Joy Butts

Director, Bookazine Development & Marketing
Laura Adam

Finance Director
Glenn Buonocore

Associate Publishing Director
Megan Pearlman

Assistant General Counsel
Helen Wan

Assistant Director, Special Sales
Ilene Schreider

Design & Prepress Manager
Anne-Michelle Gallero

Brand Manager, Product Marketing
Nina Fleishman

Associate Prepress Manager
Alex Voznesenskiy

Associate Production Manager
Kimberly Marshall

Editorial Director: Stephen Koepp
Editorial Operations Director: Michael Q. Bullerdick

General Editor: Christopher D. Hudson
Senior Editor: Kelly Knauer
Managing Editor: Carol Smith

**Consulting Editors with The Nida Institute
for Biblical Scholarship at American Bible Society:**
Philip H. Towner, Ph.D.
Barbara Bernstengel, M.A.
Robert Hodgson, Ph.D.
Charles Houser, B.A.
Davina McDonald, M.A.
Thomas May, M.Div.
*With special thanks to the American Bible Society's Committee
on Translation and Scholarship*

Contributing Writers:
Anita Palmer
Gordon Lawrence
Mia Littlejohn
Carol Smith
Randy Southern
Jessica Thomas

Design and Production:
Mark Wainwright
Symbology Creative

SPECIAL THANKS TO:
Christine Austin, Jeremy Biloon, Susan Chodakiewicz,
Rose Cirrincione, Lauren Hall Clark, Jacqueline Fitzgerald, Christine Font,
Jenna Goldberg, Hillary Hirsch, Suzanne Janso, David Kahn, Mona Li, Amy
Mangus, Robert Marasco, Amy Migliaccio, Nina Mistry, Dave Rozzelle,
Adriana Tierno, Vanessa Wu

Unless otherwise noted, all Scripture quotations are from the Holy Bible, *Contemporary English Version* (CEV). Copyright 2006 by American Bible Society. Used by permission of the American Bible Society. All rights reserved.

Scripture quotations marked NIV are taken from the Holy Bible, *New International Version*, copyright © 1973, 1978, 1984 by the International Bible Society. Used by permission of Zondervan. All rights reserved.

ISBN 10: 1-60320-946-8   ISBN 13: 978-1-60320-946-5

We welcome your comments and suggestions about Time Home Entertainment Books. Please write to us at:
Time Home Entertainment Books
Attention: Book Editors
PO Box 11016
Des Moines, IA 50336-1016

If you would like to order any of our hardcover Collector's Edition books, please call us at
1-800-327-6388, Monday through Friday, 7 a.m. to 8 p.m., or Saturday, 7 a.m. to 6 p.m., Central Time.

Table of Contents

CHAPTER 5

Heavenly Secrets: The World of Angels

**Heaven's messengers appear in a glimpse and vanish in a moment.
They wield incredible power and carry out the secret commands of God himself.**

CHAPTER 6

Strange Tales: Foretold and Fulfilled

Did the Bible provide a road map to the rise and fall of world powers?

CHAPTER 7

Unlikely Heroes: The Improbable Rise of Bible Greats

**What made so many of the Bible heroes special? What was the secret behind the
success and power of characters such as:**

CHAPTER 8

The End of the World: Unlocking the Future

What does the Bible say about the end of the world?

CHAPTER 1

The Bible:
Book of Secrets

No book is more widely read—or more hotly debated—than the Bible.
For centuries, believers and skeptics alike have tried to unlock its mysteries.

Ancient humans living for hundreds of years. A mighty sea being parted in two.
Not only ancient prophets but also Jesus himself brought people back from the dead.
Each of these miraculous events presaged the greatest miracle of all:
Jesus' resurrection from the dead.

These are but a few of the unexplained phenomena we encounter in the Bible.
Whatever we make of them, they are an indelible part of its story.
The Bible insists again and again that God has influenced human history,
and the results defy easy explanation.

The Bible challenges many of our assumptions about the world around us.
It forces us to ask:

Is there more to life
than what we can see?

Miracles:
Mystery or Hoax?

Was the entire world spoken into existence?
Did the Hebrew people really walk through the Red Sea
on dry ground?
Did Jesus heal the sick?
Could he have actually risen from the dead?

These kinds of extraordinary events appear throughout the Bible, often without explanation. The Bible doesn't set out to prove the reality of miracles. It simply assumes they're a part of life—albeit an unusual one.

For those who witnessed miracles like these, they were mysterious signs pointing to a larger meaning. When Moses, for example, stumbled across a bush that was on fire but not burning up, it not only got his attention but also made clear that the message he would be given was of special importance.

Likewise, for Jews living in first-century Palestine, Jesus' miracles revealed an authority and power the likes of which they had never seen and could not fully comprehend. The miracles of Jesus demonstrated God's love for the people (Luke 4:18–21) and announced the imminent arrival of the kingdom of God (Matthew 12:28).

For the ancient Mediterranean world, miracles defied understanding and were unable to be explained by known expectations of how nature works. Miracles got people's attention, motivating them to consider their source. The events themselves did not create faith but were often performed for those who already had faith—who believed in spite of mystery and uncertainty.

As we read about these miracles today, they invite us to consider a mysterious power beyond ourselves.

A Reading from Deuteronomy 4:35–36

The LORD wants you to know he is the only true God, and he wants you to obey him.
That's why he let you see his mighty miracles and his fierce fire on earth,
and why you heard his voice from that fire and from the sky.

READ IT FOR YOURSELF

DEUTERONOMY 29:2–6

Moses called the nation of Israel together and told them:
"When you were in Egypt, you saw the LORD perform great miracles that caused trouble for the king, his officials, and everyone else in the country. He has even told you, 'For 40 years I, the LORD, led you through the desert, but your clothes and your sandals didn't wear out, and I gave you special food. I did these things so you would realize that I am your God.' But the LORD must give you a change of heart before you truly understand what you have seen and heard."

EXODUS 34:10

The LORD said:
"I promise to perform miracles for you that have never been seen anywhere on earth. Neighboring nations will stand in fear and know that I was the one who did these marvelous things."

1 CHRONICLES 16:11–12

Trust the LORD
and his mighty power.
   Worship him always.
Remember his miracles
and all his wonders
   and his fair decisions.

painting above:
Moses at the top of Mt. Horeb holding up his arms
during the battle, assisted by Aaron and Hur
John Everett Millais

JOB 37:4–7

God's majestic voice thunders his
commands, creating miracles
too marvelous for us to understand.
Snow and heavy rainstorms make us
stop and think about God's power.

Jesus worked many other miracles for his disciples, and not all of them are written in this book. But these are written so that you will put your faith in Jesus as the Messiah and the Son of God. If you have faith in him, you will have true life.
— John 20:30–31

Fascination with the Unexplained

Why are people fascinated with the mysteries of the Bible?

Nearly two millennia after the formation of the Bible as we know it today was finalized, the quest to understand its mysteries continues unabated, perhaps because they provide a glimpse into a world beyond the one we can see and experience.

The thrill we feel when confronted by a supernatural mystery is a bit like the thrill a child experiences when being told an exciting secret. We feel the rush of adrenaline as we encounter something few can understand—or the suspense of not knowing what will happen next. Confronted with the prospect of someone who isn't bound by the laws of nature, we might even feel a bit of uncertainty or fear. We begin to suspect there is something beyond what we can observe with our five senses.

The Bible is a book that raises many questions (and offers a few answers) about the supernatural world. While those who experienced these extraordinary events described throughout this book held a different perspective on them than the perspective of a modern world, their stories still speak to us, even if we don't fully understand them. In this modern world where we have so many answers at our fingertips, these events remind us that mystery is a part of life and faith.

READ IT FOR YOURSELF

MARK 16:20

Then the disciples left and preached everywhere. The Lord was with them, and the miracles they worked proved that their message was true.

ACTS 14:3

Paul and Barnabas stayed there for a while, having faith in the Lord and bravely speaking his message. The Lord gave them the power to work miracles and wonders, and he showed that their message about his gift of undeserved grace was true.

A Reading from Mark 9:14–24

When Jesus and his three disciples came back down, they saw a large crowd around the other disciples. The teachers of the Law of Moses were arguing with them.

The crowd was really surprised to see Jesus, and everyone hurried over to greet him.

Jesus asked, "What are you arguing about?"

Someone from the crowd answered, "Teacher, I brought my son to you. A demon keeps him from talking. Whenever the demon attacks my son, it throws him to the ground and makes him foam at the mouth and grit his teeth in pain. Then he becomes stiff. I asked your disciples to force out the demon, but they couldn't do it."

Jesus said, "You people don't have any faith! How much longer must I be with you? Why do I have to put up with you? Bring the boy to me."

They brought the boy, and as soon as the demon saw Jesus, it made the boy shake all over. He fell down and began rolling on the ground and foaming at the mouth.

Jesus asked the boy's father, "How long has he been like this?"

The man answered, "Ever since he was a child. The demon has often tried to kill him by throwing him into a fire or into water. Please have pity and help us if you can!"

Jesus replied, "Why do you say 'if you can'? Anything is possible for someone who has faith!"

At once the boy's father shouted, "I do have faith! Please help me to have even more."

image above:
Evangeliar der Äbtissin Hitda von Meschede, Szene: Jesus und die Schwiegermutter Petri (Jesus Healing Peter's Mother-in-Law)
Meister des Hitda-Evangeliars

Miracles of the Bible

A partial list of miracles found in the Bible:

EXODUS 3

- God appeared to Moses in a bush that was on fire but did not burn up.

EXODUS 7–12

- Egypt was struck with ten devastating plagues when its king refused to free the Hebrew slaves.

EXODUS 14

- The waters of the Red Sea were parted so that the Hebrews could walk through it after their escape from Egypt.

EXODUS 16

- God miraculously fed the Hebrews as they wandered in the desert.

JOSHUA 6

- The walls of Jericho collapsed when the Israelite soldiers marched around the city and shouted as loud as they could.

1 KINGS 17

- A prophet named Elijah raised a widow's dead son back to life.

1 KINGS 18

- In a dramatic confrontation with the prophets of Baal, Elijah called down fire to consume his offering to God—on an altar that was soaking wet.

2 KINGS 5

- A Syrian military commander named Naaman was cured of leprosy when he washed in the Jordan River.

JONAH 1–2

- A prophet named Jonah was swallowed by a big fish and lived to tell the story.

DANIEL 3

- Shadrach, Meshach, and Abednego survived being thrown into a fiery furnace after refusing to obey the Babylonian king's order to worship a gold statue.

DANIEL 6

- Daniel was thrown into a pit of lions but an angel kept the lions from eating him.

MATTHEW 8; MARK 1; LUKE 5

- Jesus cured a man of leprosy.

MATTHEW 9; MARK 5; LUKE 8

- A woman with a mysterious bleeding disorder was healed when she touched Jesus' clothes.

MARK 8

- Jesus restored sight to a blind man by spitting into his eyes.

MATTHEW 14; MARK 6; LUKE 9; JOHN 6

- Jesus miraculously fed 5,000 men, plus many women and children.

MATTHEW 14; MARK 6; JOHN 6

- Jesus terrified his disciples by walking on water.

MATTHEW 28; MARK 16; LUKE 24; JOHN 20

- Jesus rose from the dead after dying on a cross.

JOHN 11

- Jesus raised Lazarus, who had been dead four days, to life.

ACTS 3

- Peter and John healed a man who had been born lame.

MIRACLES: SIGNPOSTS OF THE DIVINE

The word *miracle* usually brings to mind that which is thought impossible—that which defies understanding and contravenes the laws of nature. But the reason for a miracle is just as important as its occurrence.

Many miracles recorded in the Hebrew Scriptures are understood to be signs of God's judgment—such as the ten plagues of Egypt. Other miracles were acts of deliverance. After leaving Egypt, for example, the Hebrews crossed the dry bed of a parted sea and ate a steady diet of miraculously supplied food. There were also great escapes, like Daniel's deliverance from a pit of lions and the protection of his companions in the fiery furnace.

The New Testament records many healing miracles, both during the ministry of Jesus and later by his disciples. Those who were paralyzed walked again. The dead came back to life. Jesus also performed miracles to provide for people's most basic needs—multiplying food and calming storms, for example.

We may not understand how miracles could possibly happen, but a deeper truth lies behind their mystery. If the Bible's miraculous accounts are true, then they point to a God who is not far removed from us, but who is intimately involved in our world—a God who cares deeply about humanity. Miracles are a sign of the divine at work in our midst.

The Crossing of the Red Sea
Marc Chagall

Jesus: Secret Ambition or Prophetic Fulfillment?

After their kingdom's collapse and the fall of Jerusalem in the sixth century BC, Israelite hope hinged on a single word: Messiah.

The Messiah, or Chosen One, would deliver his people—and all humanity—from bondage. He would restore the broken line of kings descended from Israel's greatest ruler, David. He would break the yoke of oppression.

But the Messiah was shrouded in mystery. No one knew when he would come or who he would be.

At the turn of the ages, an itinerant preacher named Jesus began drawing attention with his provocative teachings and powerful miracles. Over time, many wondered if Jesus was the long-awaited Messiah. His very name meant "to deliver," embodying the hope of his people.

Was it Jesus' ambition to rescue his people and reclaim David's throne? Did he plan his path to kingship, or was he destined from the start to play this role?

Messiah:
Mysterious Promise

The hope of the Hebrew Scriptures hung on a mysterious promise foretold by ancient prophets: someday a deliverer would rescue humanity from sin and despair. But when? And who?

Unlocking the messianic secret was not easy. Sometimes political circumstances forced the prophets to speak in language so cryptic that the full impact of their words would only be discovered centuries later.

Still, an unexpectedly specific picture emerges from the cloud of mystery. Prophets like Isaiah and Micah described the Messiah's coming in startling detail: what kind of man he would be, where he would be born, and the circumstances that would herald his advent.

The authors of the four canonical New Testament Gospels—books that tell the good news of Jesus Christ and are the primary source of biographical information about him—noted the many connections between the prophets of old and the first-century world in which Jesus lived and taught. Matthew, in particular, often referred to the prophets of the Hebrew Scriptures. His first readers were Jewish and would have been well acquainted with the prophetic tradition that receives such strong emphasis in Matthew's Gospel.

Whether directly quoting the prophets or simply alluding to them, the Gospel writers saw their predecessors' words as confirmation that Jesus was, in fact, the Messiah that Israel had been waiting for.

Modern-day Bethlehem

ANNA

The prophets of the Bible include some surprising characters, like an 84-year-old widow named Anna, who prophesied a few days after Jesus' birth. Luke's Gospel tells her story in just a few sentences. Anna had been married only seven years when her husband died. Apparently, she remained single the rest of her life, serving God in the temple, praying, and fasting. Luke says she was at the temple *"night and day."*

On the day the infant Jesus was brought to the temple to be presented —as was the custom then—a man named Simeon recognized Jesus as the fulfillment of God's promise to send someone to save his people (see Luke 2:29–32).

Upon hearing Simeon's proclamation, Anna began to spread the word about Jesus to those who *"hoped for Jerusalem to be set free"* (Luke 2:36–38).

READ IT FOR YOURSELF

MICAH 5:2

Bethlehem Ephrath,
you are one of the smallest towns
   in the nation of Judah.
But the LORD will choose
one of your people
   to rule the nation—
someone whose family
   goes back to ancient times.

The Adoration of the Shepherds, 1505–1510
Giorgione

Prophecies of a King

Early Prophecies of Deliverance

Some early Christians regarded the Bible's first promise of a Messiah to be the direct result of the fall into sin. After a snake convinced humankind's first couple to disobey God's command, God revealed that a descendant of Eve would be sent to deal with the snake once and for all (Genesis 3:15). Christian tradition has long viewed this cryptic statement as the earliest reference to a Messiah who would fight back against the power of sin, as personified by the snake (Revelation 12:7–9).

Later, the prophet Isaiah foretold that a virgin would become miraculously pregnant and give birth to a son (Isaiah 7:14)—not just any son, but a son named Immanuel, or "God is with us."

Two Gospel writers identified Mary, the mother of Jesus, as the ultimate fulfillment of this prophecy (Matthew 1:18–23; Luke 1:26–38).

Yet another prophet, Micah, foretold that Israel's Savior would come from the obscure town of Bethlehem (located about six miles south of Jerusalem). He would rule the nation of Israel, according to Micah, and bring peace (Micah 5:2–6). Centuries later, Matthew provided the last piece of the puzzle, declaring that Jesus was the mysterious deliverer of whom Micah spoke (Matthew 2:1, 5–6).

These three prophecies, among others, indicate how the followers of Jesus understood God's mysterious plan of salvation as it unfolded in the life of Jesus. They provided clues that ordinary people living centuries later would use to identify the Messiah they'd been waiting for.

READ IT FOR YOURSELF

LUKE 1:26–27

One month later God sent the angel Gabriel to the town of Nazareth in Galilee with a message for a virgin named Mary. She was engaged to Joseph from the family of King David.

17

A Royal Bloodline

The Messianic Hope, from Abraham to Jesus

ABRAHAM

While the Israelites waited for their hoped-for Messiah, they clung to promises God had made to their ancestors long ago.

God promised the elderly Abraham, the great patriarch of the Israelites, that he would father many nations and that God would bless the entire world through his descendants (Genesis 12:1–3; 22:16–18).

Just two generations later, God's promise was repeated to Abraham's grandson Jacob: *"Your descendants will spread over the earth in all directions and will become as numerous as the specks of dust. Your family will be a blessing to all people"* (Genesis 28:14).

But exactly how would God use Abraham's descendants to bless the world? It was the Gospel according to Matthew (1:2) and the apostle Paul, whose letters would one day be included in the New Testament, that solved this puzzle by connecting Jesus to God's covenant with Abraham. *"The promises were not made to many descendants,"* Paul wrote, *"but only to one, and that one is Christ"* (Galatians 3:16). Paul recognized Jesus as a descendant of Abraham—and therefore, as the fulfillment of God's promise of salvation to Abraham, his descendants, and everyone on earth.

READ IT FOR YOURSELF

GENESIS 12:1–3

The LORD said to Abram: "Leave your country, your family, and your relatives and go to the land that I will show you. I will bless you and make your descendants into a great nation. You will become famous and be a blessing to others. I will bless those who bless you, but I will put a curse on anyone who puts a curse on you. Everyone on earth will be blessed because of you."

Abraham's Journey from Ur to Canaan, 1850
József Molnár

HEROD AND THE KING OF THE JEWS

Slaughter of the Innocents, 1304–1306, Giotto

Jesus' claim to David's throne set him on a collision course with Herod, the Roman-backed ruler of Judea. Herod sensed a threat when a group of wise men—people who studied the stars—visited him, asking where the promised *"king of the Jews"* could be found.

Any potential rival had to be exterminated, as far as Herod was concerned. So he consulted Jewish religious authorities to unravel the mystery of the Messiah's birth. Quoting Micah 5:2, the religious leaders told Herod the Messiah would be born in Bethlehem.

Herod ordered the massacre of all the male infants in Bethlehem. Jesus and his family escaped, but this sad tale fulfilled yet another prophecy (Jeremiah 31:15) connected to the Messiah (see Matthew 2:1–18).

KING DAVID

The story of Israel's greatest king unlocks yet another mystery about the coming of the promised Messiah.

While God promised to bless Abraham, his covenant with David promised the king that his royal dynasty would never end. God said to David, *"I will make sure that one of your descendants will always be king"* (2 Samuel 7:16; see also Psalms 89:3–4; 132:11; Isaiah 11:1; Jeremiah 23:5). This promise was confirmed when the angel told Mary that her son *"will be great,"* that *"the Lord God will make him king, as his ancestor David was,"* and that *"his kingdom will never end"* (Luke 1:32–33).

This posed a mysterious dilemma after Israel's collapse in 586 BC. How could David be father of a never-ending dynasty if his throne sat empty? The prophets answered this riddle by declaring that the Messiah would sit on David's throne. According to Christian tradition, Isaiah's words pointed to the future Messiah: *"A child has been born for us. We have been given a son who will be our ruler. His names will be Wonderful Advisor and Mighty God, Eternal Father and Prince of Peace. His power will never end; peace will last forever. He will rule David's kingdom and make it grow strong. He will always rule with honesty and justice. The* LORD *All-Powerful will make certain that all of this is done"* (Isaiah 9:6–7).

The Israelites expected their Messiah to be both a descendant of Abraham and heir to David's throne. Matthew's and Luke's Gospels both include genealogies tracing Jesus' bloodline to David (Matthew 1:1–17; Luke 3:23–38). This was their way of revealing to their readers that Jesus was the promised Messiah foretold by the prophets of the Hebrew Scriptures. Luke's genealogy concludes by revealing an even greater mystery about the Messiah; Luke designates Jesus as the Son of God.

READ IT FOR YOURSELF

PSALM 89:3–4

You said, "David, my servant,
  is my chosen one,
  and this is the agreement
  I made with him:
David, one of your descendants
  will always be king."

MATTHEW 1:1a, 17

Jesus Christ came from the family of King David and also from the family of Abraham....There were 14 generations from Abraham to David. There were also 14 from David to the exile in Babylonia and 14 more to the birth of the Messiah.

The Miraculous

Healing the Blind, Deaf, Lame, Mute . . . and Fulfilling Prophecy

The prophet Isaiah promised a Messiah who would do the impossible. The Gospels attribute many miracles to Jesus, using them to underscore his identity as the Messiah, Israel's long-awaited king and deliverer.

Unlike most kings, Jesus used his power to benefit others—and to reveal the mystery of God's presence among them. The miracles of Jesus reinforced the prophets' vision of a deliverer who would repair what was broken, heal the wounded, and restore the lost.

Yet there were times when Jesus refused to do miracles. He pushed back against those who simply wanted a sign, a gimmick designed to impress them into believing. An even greater mystery is the Gospels' claim that there were some places where Jesus could not perform many miracles because the inhabitants lacked faith.

Nevertheless, it was Jesus' miraculous activity—combined with the authority with which he spoke—that made people around him take notice and realize this was no ordinary man living among them, gathering followers, and offering hope. The miracles of Jesus led many to ponder the mystery of his true identity.

Christ Rescuing Peter from Drowning, 1370
Lorenzo Veneziano
Staatliche Museen, Berlin

THE MIRACLES OF JESUS

WATER TURNED INTO WINE: JOHN 2:1–11

THE OFFICIAL'S SON: JOHN 4:46–54

THE GREAT HAUL OF FISH: LUKE 5:1–11

A MAN WITH AN EVIL SPIRIT: MARK 1:23–28; LUKE 4:33–37

PETER'S MOTHER-IN-LAW: MATTHEW 8:14–15; MARK 1:29–31; LUKE 4:38–39

THE LEPER: MATTHEW 8:1–4; MARK 1:40–45; LUKE 5:12–16

THE PARALYTIC CURED: MATTHEW 9:1–8; MARK 2:1–12; LUKE 5:17–26

THE CURE AT BETHZATHA: JOHN 5:1–15

THE MAN WITH A PARALYZED HAND: MATTHEW 12:9–13; MARK 3:1–6; LUKE 6:6–11

THE ARMY OFFICIAL'S SERVANT: MATTHEW 8:5–13; LUKE 7:1–10

THE WIDOW'S SON: LUKE 7:11–17

THE BLIND AND MUTE DEMONIAC: MATTHEW 12:22

THE STORM STILLED: MATTHEW 8:23–27; MARK 4:35–41; LUKE 8:22–25

EXPULSION OF DEMONS: MATTHEW 8:28–34; MARK 5:1–20; LUKE 8:26–39

JAIRUS'S DAUGHTER: MATTHEW 9:18–26; MARK 5:21–43; LUKE 8:40–56

THE WOMAN IN THE CROWD: MATTHEW 9:20–22; MARK 5:25–34; LUKE 8:43–48

TWO BLIND MEN: MATTHEW 9:27–31

THE MUTE SPIRIT: MATTHEW 9:32–34

FIVE THOUSAND FED: MATTHEW 14:13–21; MARK 6:30–44; LUKE 9:10–17; JOHN 6:1–15

JESUS WALKS ON THE WATER: MATTHEW 14:22–33; MARK 6:45–52; JOHN 6:16–21

THE CANAANITE WOMAN: MATTHEW 15:21–28; MARK 7:24–30

THE DEAF MUTE: MARK 7:31–37

FOUR THOUSAND FED: MATTHEW 15:32–39; MARK 8:1–10

THE BLIND MAN: MARK 8:22–26

THE POSSESSED BOY: MATTHEW 17:14–21; MARK 9:14–29; LUKE 9:37–43

TRIBUTE MONEY PROVIDED: MATTHEW 17:24–27

THE MAN BORN BLIND: JOHN 9:1–41

THE MUTE, LAME, AND BLIND: MATTHEW 15:29–31

A CRIPPLED WOMAN CURED: LUKE 13:10–17

THE MAN WITH SWOLLEN LEGS: LUKE 14:1–6

THE RAISING OF LAZARUS: JOHN 11:1–44

TEN LEPERS: LUKE 17:11–19

THE BLIND MEN AT JERICHO: MATTHEW 20:29–34; MARK 10:46–52; LUKE 18:35–43

THE FIG TREE CURSED: MATTHEW 21:18–22; MARK 11:12–14, 20–26

THE SERVANT'S EAR HEALED: LUKE 22:49–51

A CATCH OF 153 FISH: JOHN 21:1–14

PROPHETIC COUNTDOWN: UNLOCKING THE MESSIANIC MYSTERY OF THE HEBREW SCRIPTURES

Listed below are selected Bible prophecies that Christians have interpreted as referring to the Messiah. In the left-hand column, you'll find the reference to the prophecy. In the right-hand column, you'll find a reference to its fulfillment. This list maintains the order in which the prophecies appear in the Bible.

PROPHECY	WHAT THE PROPHECY REVEALS ABOUT THE MESSIAH	FULFILLMENT
Genesis 3:15	He will be the offspring of a woman and defeat Satan.	Galatians 4:4–5; Revelation 12:11
Genesis 12:1–3 (see also Genesis 21:12; 22:18)	He will be a descendant of Abraham and Isaac.	Matthew 1:1, 17; Galatians 3:16; Hebrews 11:17–19
Exodus 12:46 (see also Psalm 34:20)	He will not have any of his bones broken.	John 19:33, 36
Deuteronomy 18:15–18	He will be a prophet like Moses.	Acts 3:20–22
Psalm 2:1–2, 6–7	He will be opposed by both Jews and Gentiles. He will be King of Zion and the Son of God.	Luke 1:32, 35; 23:10–12; John 18:33–37; Acts 4:27
Psalm 16:10 (see also Psalm 30:3)	His body will not decay in the grave.	Luke 24:6, 31, 34; Acts 2:31
Psalm 22:1–18	He will be forsaken by God, mocked by people, and have his clothing divided by the casting of dice.	Matthew 27:39–44, 46; Luke 22:63–65; John 19:18–20, 23–24; Romans 15:3
Psalm 41:9 (see also Psalm 55:12–14)	He will be betrayed by a friend.	Matthew 26:14–16; Mark 14:10–11; Luke 22:1–6; John 13:18, 21–30
Psalm 47:5	He will ascend into heaven.	Luke 24:51; Acts 1:9
Psalm 69:4	He will be rejected and hated for his works.	Matthew 13:57; Mark 6:4; Luke 4:24; John 1:11; 7:3–5; 15:24–25
Psalm 69:9	He will have great love for the Lord's house.	John 2:17
Psalm 69:21	He will be offered gall and vinegar to drink.	Matthew 27:34; Mark 15:36; Luke 23:36; John 19:29–30
Psalm 72:10–11 (see also Psalm 72:8; Daniel 7:14)	He will be adored by great people. He will have universal dominion.	Matthew 2:1–11; Philippians 2:9, 11
Psalm 78:2	He will preach in parables.	Matthew 13:34–35; Mark 4:33–34
Psalm 110:1 (see also Psalm 2:7; 110:4)	He will sit at the right hand of God. He will serve in Melchizedek's order of priests.	Colossians 3:1; Hebrews 1:3; 5:5–6
Psalm 118:22	He will be rejected by Jewish rulers.	Matthew 21:42; Mark 12:10; Luke 20:17; 1 Peter 2:4–7
Isaiah 7:14	He will be born of a virgin.	Matthew 1:21–23; Luke 1:34–35; 2:7
Isaiah 8:14	He will be a stumbling block to those who refuse to believe in him.	Luke 2:34; Romans 9:32–33; 1 Peter 2:8
Isaiah 9:1–2, 7 (see also Daniel 7:14)	He will have a ministry that begins in Galilee. He will have an everlasting kingdom.	Matthew 4:12–16, 23; Luke 1:32–33
Isaiah 11:10; 42:1 (see also Isaiah 56:6–8)	He will have Gentile followers.	John 10:16; Acts 10:34–35, 45, 47
Isaiah 28:16	He will be the chief cornerstone of God's people.	1 Peter 2:6–7

PROPHECY	WHAT THE PROPHECY REVEALS ABOUT THE MESSIAH	FULFILLMENT
Isaiah 35:5–6	He will perform miracles.	Matthew 11:4–6; John 9:6–7
Isaiah 40:3 (see also Malachi 3:1)	He will be preceded by an anointed messenger.	Matthew 3:13; Mark 1:2–3; Luke 1:17, 76–77; 3:3–6; John 1:23
Isaiah 42:1–6	He will be meek and speak out for justice.	Matthew 12:15–21
Isaiah 50:6 (see also Isaiah 52:14)	He will be spat on and beaten.	Matthew 26:67; Mark 14:65; 15:19; Luke 22:63; John 19:1–5
Isaiah 53:1–12	He will be condemned as a sinner and will suffer. He will be silent before his accusers (and later intercede for them), and be buried with the rich.	Matthew 26:62–63; 27:11–14, 27–50, 57–60; Mark 15:4–5, 21–37, 42–46; Luke 23:6–9, 32–46, 50–54; John 19:16–30, 38–42; 1 Peter 2:22–23
Isaiah 61:1 (see also Isaiah 11:2)	He will be anointed by the Spirit of God.	Matthew 3:16; Mark 1:10; Luke 3:22; 4:16–19; John 3:34; 5:30; Acts 10:38; Revelation 19:11
Isaiah 61:1–2	He will enter public ministry.	Luke 4:16–21, 43
Jeremiah 23:5–6 (see also Jeremiah 33:14–16)	He will be a descendant of David.	Matthew 1:1, 17; Acts 13:22–23; Romans 1:3
Jeremiah 31:15	He will be alive during the slaughter of Bethlehem's children.	Matthew 2:16–18
Hosea 11:1	He will be called out of Egypt.	Matthew 2:15
Micah 5:2–5	He will be born in Bethlehem.	Matthew 2:1–6; Luke 2:4–7
Malachi 3:1	He will arrive at Jerusalem's temple.	Matthew 21:12; Mark 11:11; Luke 19:45–48; John 2:13–16
Zechariah 9:9	He will enter Jerusalem by riding a donkey.	Matthew 21:1–5
Zechariah 11:12–13	He will be betrayed for thirty pieces of silver, which will later buy a potter's field.	Matthew 26:15; 27:7
Zechariah 12:10	He will be pierced.	John 19:34, 37
Zechariah 13:7	He will be forsaken by his disciples.	Matthew 26:31, 56; Mark 14:27, 50

A Reading from John 19:23–24

After the soldiers had nailed Jesus to the cross, they divided up his clothes into four parts, one for each of them. But his outer garment was made from a single piece of cloth, and it did not have any seams.

The soldiers said to each other, "Let's not rip it apart. We will gamble to see who gets it." This happened so that the Scriptures would come true, which say: "They divided up my clothes and gambled for my garments." The soldiers then did what they had decided.

Death and Resurrection:
What Happened to Jesus?

*"My God, my God, why have you deserted me? Why are you so far away?
Won't you listen to my groans and come to my rescue?"* (Psalm 22:1).

Psalm 22 echoes the abandonment Jesus experienced while hanging
on the cross. Jesus actually quoted this psalm during his crucifixion
(Matthew 27:46; Mark 15:34). In the same Scripture passage, we find
a clue that Jesus' clothes would be divided among his enemies (Psalm
22:18; John 19:23–24). Elsewhere, the prophet Amos described a day
when God would mysteriously darken the earth at noon—something that
occurred on the day of Jesus' death (Amos 8:9; Matthew 27:45; Mark
15:33; Luke 23:44–45).

Jesus' startling words of
forgiveness were predicted by
the prophet Isaiah (Isaiah 53:12b;
Luke 23:34). His crucifixion
alongside two criminals was also
foreseen by Isaiah (Isaiah 53:12;
Matthew 27:38; Mark 15:27;
Luke 23:32; John 19:18).

Even the events surrounding the
aftermath of Jesus' death were a
fulfillment of prophecy. Normally,
those crucified as criminals were
buried apart from respectable
citizens. Yet all four Gospels reveal
still another mystery surrounding
Jesus' death: he was buried in a
rich man's tomb. This too was in
fulfillment of ancient prophecy
(Isaiah 53:9; Matthew 27:57–60;
Mark 15:42–46; Luke 23:50–53;
John 19:38–42).

The Entombment of Christ, 1602–1604
Caravaggio

His Resurrection

No detail of Jesus' story is more startling and mysterious than his resurrection. While it is possible to uncover foreshadowings of this event by studying the prophecies of the Hebrew Scriptures, Jesus' triumph over the grave astounded even those closest to him.

The idea that death could be defeated is perhaps the Bible's greatest paradox. It is first introduced in the Garden of Eden account found in the Hebrew Scriptures (Genesis 3:15). Adam and Eve defied God's command and were expelled from paradise. God explained to each of them, and to the serpent who tempted them, that the eventual consequences of their choices would include death. But also included was a cryptic prophecy that a descendant of Adam and Eve would make right what had gone so wrong. The sin of Adam—and its consequences—would be undone by a kind of second Adam who would restore the broken bond between God and his people (see Romans 5:12–21; 1 Corinthians 15:20–22). This is not to say that Jesus and Adam were equal opposites, only that understanding the significance of Adam's fall reveals the ultimate secret of Jesus' sacrifice.

The story of Jonah provides another allusion to the Messiah's death and resurrection. Just as Jonah spent three days in the belly of a large fish, Jesus spent three days in the grave. Likewise, Jonah's deliverance from the fish mirrors Jesus' resurrection from the grave (see Jonah 1:17).

Elsewhere, both the psalmist and the prophet Isaiah claimed God would not let his chosen one remain in death's grip. Instead, God would raise him from the grave and restore him to a position of honor at God's right hand (Psalm 16:10–11; Isaiah 53:11–12).

A Reading from Romans 5:12–21

Adam sinned, and that sin brought death into the world. Now everyone has sinned, and so everyone must die. Sin was in the world before the Law came. But no record of sin was kept, because there was no Law. Yet death still had power over all who lived from the time of Adam to the time of Moses. This happened, though not everyone disobeyed a direct command from God, as Adam did.

In some ways Adam is like Christ who came later. But the gift of God's undeserved grace was very different from Adam's sin. That one sin brought death to many others. Yet in an even greater way, Jesus Christ alone brought God's gift of undeserved grace to many people.

There is a lot of difference between Adam's sin and God's gift. That one sin led to punishment. But God's gift made it possible for us to be acceptable to him, even though we have sinned many times. Death ruled like a king because Adam had sinned. But that cannot compare with what Jesus Christ has done. God has treated us with undeserved grace, and he has accepted us because of Jesus. And so we will live and rule like kings.

Everyone was going to be punished because Adam sinned. But because of the good thing that Christ has done, God accepts us and gives us the gift of life. Adam disobeyed God and caused many others to be sinners. But Jesus obeyed him and will make many people acceptable to God.

The Law came, so that the full power of sin could be seen. Yet where sin was powerful, God's gift of undeserved grace was even more powerful. Sin ruled by means of death. But God's gift of grace now rules, and God has accepted us because of Jesus Christ our Lord. This means that we will have eternal life.

Replica of the tomb

Stone of Unction inside Holy Sepulchre

Church of the Holy Sepulchre in the Old City of Jerusalem

READ IT FOR YOURSELF

PSALM 16:10–11

I am your chosen one.
You won't leave me in the grave
    or let my body decay.
You have shown me
    the path to life,
    and you make me glad
    by being near to me.
Sitting at your right side,
    I will always be joyful.

The Three Marys at the Tomb
Adolphe William Bouguereau (c. 1825–1905)

The Fall of Nineveh
John Martin (1789–1854)

CHAPTER 3

Outlandish Destructions?

The plagues of Egypt. The desolation of Jericho. These and many other events recorded in the Hebrew Scriptures depict a sometimes calamitous deity whose power and might are not to be trifled with.

Mysteriously, the same God who brings life and healing is said to rain judgment and devastation on his enemies.

In Exodus, God brings the mighty nation of Egypt to its knees. In Joshua, he wipes the city of Jericho off the map—literally. He even freezes time so the Israelites can vanquish their enemies.

God, the Bible seems to say, should not be taken lightly. But is there a method to these terrifying acts of judgment?

Can the mystery of divine judgment be deciphered, or is its secret locked away in the unfathomable depths of divine counsel?

The Plunder of Egypt

The ten plagues were a cosmic confrontation between the God of the Hebrews and Pharaoh the Egyptian king, himself worshiped as a god; this is the key to unlocking their secret.

These calamities were brought on Egypt to convince Pharaoh to release his Hebrew slaves. Moses served as God's liaison to the Egyptian ruler. Mysteriously, Pharaoh's magicians were able to imitate some of the wonders performed by Moses (Exodus 7:10–13, 20–23); but with each new plague, God's power loomed larger over the Egyptians. Soon Pharaoh's magicians could only look with awe and say, *"God has done this"* (Exodus 8:19).

The suffering brought about by the first nine plagues was immense, yet it was still not enough to convince Pharaoh to release the Hebrews. The tenth plague, however, was so devastating that he finally relented. The final plague brought the death of the firstborn son of each family in Egypt. The Israelites were spared when they placed the blood of a sacrificial lamb on the doorposts of their houses—and thus they were passed over by the enigmatic *"angel that brings death"* (Exodus 12:23). This miracle is remembered in the Jewish festival of the Passover. Christians later connected the sacrificial death of Jesus with the Passover festival, calling Jesus *"the Lamb of God"* (John 1:29), who shed his blood to offer eternal life to the world.

A Reading from
Exodus 12:23, 29–33

During that night the LORD will go through the country of Egypt and kill the first-born son in every Egyptian family. He will see where you have put the blood, and he will not come into your house. His angel that brings death will pass over and not kill your first-born sons. . . .

At midnight the LORD killed the first-born son of every Egyptian family, from the son of the king to the son of every prisoner in jail. He also killed the first-born male of every animal that belonged to the Egyptians. That night the king, his officials, and everyone else in Egypt got up and started crying bitterly. In every Egyptian home, someone was dead.

During the night the king sent for Moses and Aaron and told them, "Get your people out of my country and leave us alone! Go and worship the LORD, as you have asked. Take your sheep, goats, and cattle, and get out. But ask your God to be kind to me." The Egyptians did everything they could to get the Israelites to leave their country as quickly as possible. They said, "Please hurry and leave. If you don't, we will all be dead."

THE FIRST NINE PLAGUES RECORDED IN EXODUS WERE AS FOLLOWS:

one	The Nile and other water sources in Egypt turned into blood, killing the fish and animals that depended on them (7:14–25).
two	An infestation of frogs descended on the land (8:1–15).
three	A swarm of lice or gnats tormented the people and their animals (8:16–19).
four	Flies invaded Egypt in such unbearable numbers that people could not go anywhere without encountering them (8:20–32).
five	Disease infected the Egyptians' livestock (9:1–7).
six	Painful boils afflicted the Egyptians themselves (9:8–12).
seven	Hail mixed with thunder and lightning on the land (9:13–35).
eight	A swarm of locusts appeared, devouring the crops (10:1–20).
nine	A plague of darkness obscured the sun—a devastating assault on Egypt's most revered deity, the sun god Ra (10:21–29).

The Walls of Jericho

The siege of Jericho was the Israelites' first major victory in what was to become their homeland—but significantly, it didn't come about by their own power.

Before crossing the Jordan River to begin the assault, Israel's leader, Joshua, sent two spies to Jericho for reconnaissance. Trying to elude capture, the spies took refuge in the home of a prostitute named Rahab. In return for this protection, the Israelites agreed not to harm her and her family. Jericho, she revealed, was terrified of Israel's impending assault—even though the city was enclosed within strong walls that served as a powerful fortification.

At the start of the siege, God told the Israelite army to march around the city once a day for six days. On the seventh day, the procession marched around Jericho seven times, after which the priests of Israel blew their trumpets and the soldiers shouted out loud. The great mystery of Jericho is that its walls apparently collapsed at the sound— without the Israelites laying their siege implements to a single brick. God himself is said to have been the power by which the walls fell. Israel's army was able to charge into the city unimpeded.

The Israelites reduced the city of Jericho into a ruined heap. Only Rahab and her family were spared; her house was the only part of the wall left standing.

A Reading from Joshua 6:12–25

Early the next morning, Joshua and everyone else started marching around Jericho in the same order as the day before. One group of soldiers was in front, followed by the seven priests with trumpets and the priests who carried the chest. The rest of the army came next. The seven priests blew their trumpets while everyone marched slowly around Jericho and back to camp. They did this once a day for six days.

On the seventh day, the army got up at daybreak. They marched slowly around Jericho the same as they had done for the past six days, except on this day they went around seven times. Then the priests blew the trumpets, and Joshua yelled:

"Get ready to shout! The LORD will let you capture this town. But you must destroy it and everything in it, to show that it now belongs to the LORD. The woman Rahab helped the spies we sent. So protect her and the others who are inside her house. But kill everyone else in the town. The silver and gold and everything made of bronze and iron belong to the LORD and must be put in his treasury. Be careful to follow these instructions, because if you see something you want and take it, the LORD will destroy Israel. And it will be all your fault."

The priests blew their trumpets again, and the soldiers shouted as loud as they could. The walls of Jericho fell flat. Then the soldiers rushed up the hill, went straight into the town, and captured it. They killed everyone, men and women, young and old, everyone except Rahab and the others in her house. They even killed every cow, sheep, and donkey...

The Israelites took the silver and gold and the things made of bronze and iron and put them with the rest of the treasure that was kept at the LORD's house. Finally, they set fire to Jericho and everything in it.

(Read the full account in Joshua 5:13–6:27.)

above:
Jericho mudbrick wall

right:
The Taking of Jericho
James Tissot (1836–1902)

Secrets behind Improbable Victories:
The Day the Sun Stood Still

The book of Joshua includes many puzzling acts of judgment in which God does not merely fight against his enemies; he fights for his people. Perhaps none is as mysterious as the story of Joshua's battle with the Amorites.

King Adonizedek ruled over Jerusalem, which was not an Israelite city at this time. He called on four neighboring cities to fight alongside his army of well-trained warriors. The battle was one of the hardest that Israel faced during this era.

Joshua and the Israelite army made a surprise attack at night. The Amorite army fled in panic, after an unexpected (and abnormally fierce) hailstorm helped Israel gain the upper hand. The book of Joshua attributes the mysterious hailstorm to God's intervention on behalf of the people (Joshua 10:11).

As noon approached, Joshua asked God to do something even more amazing: make the sun and the moon stand still. Even more remarkably, God answered his prayer. The Bible itself acknowledges the powerful mystery behind this story, noting, *"Never before and never since has the LORD done anything like that for someone who prayed"* (Joshua 10:14). This miraculous victory was evidence not of Israel's prowess but of God's power.

READ IT FOR YOURSELF

JOSHUA 10:9–15

Joshua marched all night from Gilgal to Gibeon and made a surprise attack on the Amorite camp. The LORD made the enemy panic, and the Israelites started killing them right and left. They chased the Amorite troops up the road to Beth-Horon and kept on killing them, until they reached the towns of Azekah and Makkedah. And while these troops were going down through Beth-Horon Pass, the LORD made huge hailstones fall on them all the way to Azekah. More of the enemy soldiers died from the hail than from the Israelite weapons. The LORD was helping the Israelites defeat the Amorites that day. So about noon, Joshua prayed to the LORD loud enough for the Israelites to hear:

"Our LORD, make the sun stop
   in the sky over Gibeon,
and the moon stand still
   over Aijalon Valley."
So the sun and the moon
   stopped and stood still
until Israel defeated its enemies.

This poem can be found in The Book of Jashar. The sun stood still and didn't go down for about a whole day. Never before and never since has the LORD done anything like that for someone who prayed. The LORD was really fighting for Israel. After the battle, Joshua and the Israelites went back to their camp at Gilgal.

Joshua Commanding the Sun to Stand Still, 1816
John Martin

CHAPTER 4

Strange Deliverance: Unlikely Tales of Rescue and Healing

Where is God in our bleakest moments? Does he intervene or just sit idly by, letting events run their course? This is one of the oldest and deepest mysteries of faith, one that defies easy answers.

The Bible offers a strikingly relatable portrait of the human experience. Often, good people suffer while the wicked prosper, just as in our world today.

Even the Messiah was shrouded in mystery. No one knew when he would come or who he would be.

But every now and then, God breaks into the story and does something unexpected. He parts the waters of a mighty sea so a nation of slaves can escape their oppressors. He rescues three of his faithful followers from a fiery execution. He raises the dead.

What are we to make of these baffling tales of deliverance and the mysterious God behind them?

The Flood

Early in the book of Genesis, we learn that God sent a catastrophic flood, destroying almost every living thing. The scope of judgment is almost impossible to fathom. Adding to the mystery, God chose to save one man and his family. Through Noah, God preserved a remnant, sparing the world from total devastation.

On God's orders, Noah built a boat large enough to house his family and enough animals to repopulate the earth after the flood. Once the rain began to fall, it persisted forty days and nights (Genesis 7:4, 17–18)—God's judgment in tangible form.

For many, the flood is also a sign of God's desire for a new beginning. After the deluge, the rainbow became a symbol of God's promise to never again destroy the earth by flood (Genesis 9:12–17).

Perhaps the greatest secret of Noah's story is how he foreshadows another deliverer, Jesus. Both Jesus and Noah are described as people who did what was right (Genesis 6:9; 1 John 3:7). Both stand out as great deliverers—Noah saved his family from the flood, and Jesus promises to save a great multitude from a future day of judgment.

READ IT FOR YOURSELF

GENESIS 8:20–22

Noah built an altar where he could offer sacrifices to the LORD. Then he offered on the altar one of each kind of animal and bird that could be used for a sacrifice. The smell of the burning offering pleased the LORD, and he said:

"Never again will I punish the earth for the sinful things its people do. All of them have evil thoughts from the time they are young, but I will never destroy everything that breathes, as I did this time.

"As long as the earth remains, there will be planting and harvest, cold and heat; winter and summer, day and night."

40

CRACKING THE CODE: The Number Forty

Numbers in the Bible often carry symbolic meaning. Their true significance can be elusive to many readers.

The number forty, for example, often symbolizes a time of testing or trial—such as the duration of rainfall (forty days) before the flood.

Other examples are the Israelites' forty-year journey in the desert wilderness on their way to Canaan (Numbers 32:13) and Jesus' forty-day sojourn in the wilderness, during which he was tempted by Satan himself (Mark 1:13).

A Reading from Genesis 6:5–14, 17–22

The Lord saw how bad the people on earth were and that everything they thought and planned was evil. He was sorry that he had made them, and he said, "I'm going to destroy every person on earth! I'll even wipe out animals, birds, and reptiles. I'm sorry I ever made them."

But the Lord was pleased with Noah, and this is the story about him. Noah was the only person who lived right and obeyed God. He had three sons: Shem, Ham, and Japheth.

God knew that everyone was terribly cruel and violent. So he told Noah:

"Cruelty and violence have spread everywhere. Now I'm going to destroy the whole earth and all its people. Get some good lumber and build a boat. Put rooms in it and cover it with tar inside and out. . . .

"I'm going to send a flood that will destroy everything that breathes! Nothing will be left alive. But I solemnly promise that you, your wife, your sons, and your daughters-in-law will be kept safe in the boat. Take into the boat with you a male and a female of every kind of animal and bird, as well as a male and a female of every reptile. I don't want them to be destroyed. Store up enough food both for yourself and for them."

Noah did everything God told him to do.

The Israelites Leaving Egypt, 1829
David Roberts

Christ in the Desert
Ivan Nikolaevich Kramskoi (1837–1887)

Walking Through Water

For 430 years the Israelites lived as slaves in Egypt. Everything changed, however, when a man named Moses announced that the God of their ancestors—a God they barely knew—had incredible plans for them.

Moses petitioned the Egyptian king, or Pharaoh, to let the Israelites go. At first, Pharaoh was stubborn; it took ten plagues—including the death of all of Egypt's firstborn sons—to finally convince him to change his mind (see "The Plunder of Egypt"). From the beginning, Israel's journey from slavery to liberation was filled with peril.

It did not take long for Pharaoh to regret his decision to release the Israelites—once he realized that it meant a sizable loss to his labor force. Furious, the king and his forces pursued the Israelites until they finally caught up and trapped them against the shores of the Red Sea.

What happened next has become one of the most iconic and baffling miracles of the Bible. Moses stretched his walking stick over the sea, and a strong wind blew all night long, dividing the sea until the land was actually dry and the Israelites were able to walk across the seabed (Exodus 14:21–22).

This strange tale of deliverance did not end well for the Egyptian army, however. God only kept the sea parted long enough for the Israelites to pass through it. As the Egyptians continued their pursuit, God brought the parted walls of water crashing down on the pursuing Egyptian soldiers, destroying them all. With one last rush of the sea, the Israelites were finally free from more than four centuries of slavery.

A Reading from Exodus 14:15–29

The LORD said to Moses, "Why do you keep calling out to me for help? Tell the Israelites to move forward. Then hold your walking stick over the sea. The water will open up and make a road where they can walk through on dry ground. I will make the Egyptians so stubborn that they will go after you. Then I will be praised because of what happens to the king and his chariots and cavalry. The Egyptians will know for sure that I am the LORD."

All this time God's angel had gone ahead of Israel's army, but now he moved behind them. A large cloud had also gone ahead of them, but now it moved between the Egyptians and the Israelites. The cloud gave light to the Israelites, but made it dark for the Egyptians, and during the night they could not come any closer.

Moses stretched his arm over the sea, and the LORD sent a strong east wind that blew all night until there was dry land where the water had been. The sea opened up, and the Israelites walked through on dry land with a wall of water on each side.

The Egyptian chariots and cavalry went after them. But before daylight the LORD looked down at the Egyptian army from the fiery cloud and made them panic. Their chariot wheels got stuck, and it was hard for them to move. So the Egyptians said to one another, "Let's leave these people alone! The LORD is on their side and is fighting against us."

The LORD told Moses, "Stretch your arm toward the sea—the water will cover the Egyptians and their cavalry and chariots." Moses stretched out his arm, and at daybreak the water rushed toward the Egyptians. They tried to run away, but the LORD drowned them in the sea. The water came and covered the chariots, the cavalry, and the whole Egyptian army that had followed the Israelites into the sea. Not one of them was left alive. But the sea had made a wall of water on each side of the Israelites, so they walked through on dry land.

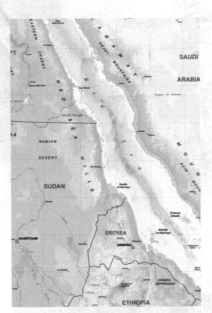

The Red Sea

Crossing of the Red Sea. Miniature from the Codex Landau-Finaly (Visconti Hours) Belbello da Pavia (c.1430–1473)

Snake on a Pole

The Brazen Serpent
Anthony van Dyck (1599–1641)

In one of the more unusual tales of deliverance, God sent poisonous snakes to punish his people. When they cried for mercy, he provided a way of deliverance. The object of healing, however, bears an uncanny resemblance to the deadly snakes.

Despite God's provision, many of the Israelites preferred their former life in Egypt to the uncertainty of the desert wilderness. Eventually, it seems that God grew tired of their persistent grumbling. According to  Numbers 21:4–9, he sent poisonous snakes, which bit and killed many Israelites. When the people admitted their error, God instructed Moses to make a bronze snake and place it on top of a pole. Anyone who looked on it would be healed.

One of the more puzzling aspects of this story is why God required the Israelites to gaze upon a replica of the very thing that was killing so many of them. Perhaps the bronze snake was intended to be a sobering reminder of their vulnerability and mortality.

A Reading from Numbers 21:4–9

The Israelites had to go around the territory of Edom, so when they left Mount Hor, they headed south toward the Red Sea. But along the way, the people became so impatient that they complained against God and said to Moses, "Did you bring us out of Egypt, just to let us die in the desert? There's no water out here, and we can't stand this awful food!"

Then the LORD sent poisonous snakes that bit and killed many of them.

Some of the people went to Moses and admitted, "It was wrong of us to insult you and the LORD. Now please ask him to make these snakes go away."

Moses prayed, and the LORD answered, "Make a snake out of bronze and place it on top of a pole. Anyone who gets bitten can look at the snake and be saved from death."

Moses obeyed the LORD. And all of those who looked at the bronze snake lived, even though they had been bitten by the poisonous snakes.

The New Testament writer John referred back to this event.

The Gospel of John refers to a conversation between Jesus and a religious leader named Nicodemus. Jesus compared the saving power of the metal snake to the death that the "Son of Man" (a term Jesus used to refer to himself) would experience in order to provide eternal life to those who believed (see John 3:14).

above: *The Brazen Serpent*
Benjamin West (1738–1820)

The Fiery Furnace

In 605 BC Nebuchadnezzar became king of Babylonia—and a power-hungry king he was. He required his citizens to worship him. He even ordered a ninety-foot-tall statue to be made from gold and put on public display. When the music began to play, everyone was ordered to fall down and worship the statue. Those who didn't were to be thrown into a fiery furnace.

Earlier in Nebuchadnezzar's reign, the Babylonians had sacked Jerusalem and carried many Jews into exile. Among the captives were Hananiah, Mishael, and Azariah (also called Shadrach, Meshach, and Abednego), three young men with a strong devotion to God. Because of their faith, they refused to worship any idol made by human hands. Such a blatant violation of the royal decree made Nebuchadnezzar furious; he ordered the furnace to be made seven times hotter than usual before having the three young men tied up and thrown in. According to the Bible, the furnace was so hot that flames leaped out and killed the soldiers who threw the men in.

Yet moments after the men were thrown into the furnace, the king noticed something terrifying—the three men were no longer tied up; they were walking around in the furnace! Even more shocking, a mysterious fourth person was walking around with them. When the king had Shadrach, Meshach, and Abednego removed from the furnace, he saw that the fire hadn't harmed them at all. Their hair wasn't burned; their clothes were intact and didn't even smell like smoke.

King Nebuchadnezzar responded by praising Israel's God for sending an angel to protect the men. He applauded their faithfulness and ordered that no people or nation ever speak against their God. The three young Jewish men who defied the king lived to tell about it.

MYSTERY MAN: THE FOURTH PERSON IN THE FURNACE

The book of Daniel never reveals the identity of the fourth person in the furnace. Nebuchadnezzar thought the mysterious individual looked "like a god." Some early Christian interpreters of this passage believed that the fourth man was Jesus—a view that was frequently depicted in early and medieval art. This story, then, would provide an unexpected glimpse of Christ before his appearance in the New Testament.

A Reading from Daniel 3:4–29

Then an official stood up and announced:

"People of every nation and race, now listen to the king's command! Trumpets, flutes, harps, and all other kinds of musical instruments will soon start playing. When you hear the music, you must bow down and worship the statue that King Nebuchadnezzar has set up. Anyone who refuses will at once be thrown into a flaming furnace."

As soon as the people heard the music, they bowed down and worshiped the gold statue that the king had set up.

Some Babylonians used this as a chance to accuse the Jews to King Nebuchadnezzar. They said, "Your Majesty, we hope you live forever! You commanded everyone to bow down and worship the gold statue when the music played. And you said that anyone who did not bow down and worship it would be thrown into a flaming furnace. Sir, you appointed three men to high positions in Babylon Province, but they have disobeyed you. Those Jews, Shadrach, Meshach, and Abednego, refuse to worship your gods and the statue you have set up."

King Nebuchadnezzar was furious. So he sent for the three young men and said, "I hear that you refuse to worship my gods and the gold statue I have set up. Now I am going to give you one more chance. If you bow down and worship the statue when you hear the music, everything will be all right. But if you don't, you will at once be thrown into a flaming furnace. No god can save you from me."

The three men replied, "Your Majesty, we don't need to defend ourselves. The God we worship can save us from you and your flaming furnace. But even if he doesn't, we still won't worship your gods and the gold statue you have set up."

Nebuchadnezzar's face twisted with anger at the three men. And he ordered the furnace to be heated seven times hotter than usual. Next,

*A Reading from
Isaiah 53:2b–8a, 10a*

*He wasn't some handsome king.
Nothing about the way he looked
made him attractive to us. He
was hated and rejected; his life
was filled with sorrow and terrible suffering. No one wanted
to look at him. We despised him
and said, "He is a nobody!"
He suffered and endured great
pain for us, but we thought
his suffering was punishment
from God. He was wounded and
crushed because of our sins; by
taking our punishment, he made
us completely well. All of us were
like sheep that had wandered
off. We had each gone our own
way, but the LORD gave him the
punishment we deserved. He was
painfully abused, but he did not
complain. He was silent like a
lamb being led to the butcher, as
quiet as a sheep having its wool
cut off. He was condemned to
death without a fair trial. Who
could have imagined what would
happen to him?*

. . .

*The LORD decided his servant
would suffer as a sacrifice to take
away the sin and guilt of others.*

Isaiah's Suffering Servant

Christ at the Column, c. 1476
Antonello da Messina (c. 1430–1479)

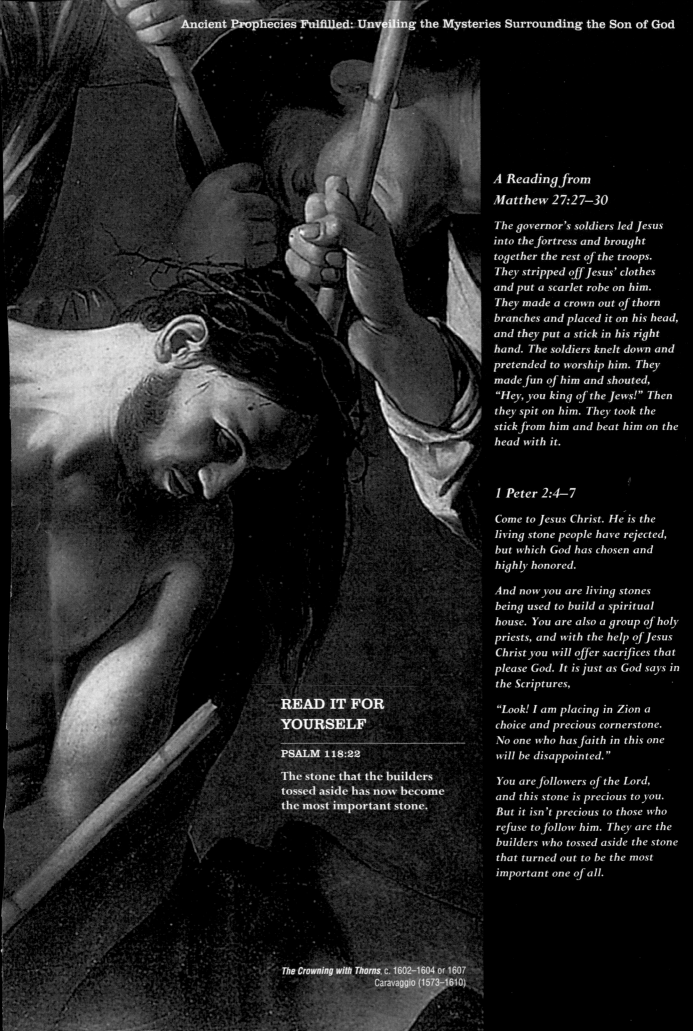

A Reading from
Matthew 27:27–30

The governor's soldiers led Jesus into the fortress and brought together the rest of the troops. They stripped off Jesus' clothes and put a scarlet robe on him. They made a crown out of thorn branches and placed it on his head, and they put a stick in his right hand. The soldiers knelt down and pretended to worship him. They made fun of him and shouted, "Hey, you king of the Jews!" Then they spit on him. They took the stick from him and beat him on the head with it.

1 Peter 2:4–7

Come to Jesus Christ. He is the living stone people have rejected, but which God has chosen and highly honored.

And now you are living stones being used to build a spiritual house. You are also a group of holy priests, and with the help of Jesus Christ you will offer sacrifices that please God. It is just as God says in the Scriptures,

"Look! I am placing in Zion a choice and precious cornerstone. No one who has faith in this one will be disappointed."

You are followers of the Lord, and this stone is precious to you. But it isn't precious to those who refuse to follow him. They are the builders who tossed aside the stone that turned out to be the most important one of all.

READ IT FOR YOURSELF

PSALM 118:22

The stone that the builders tossed aside has now become the most important stone.

The Crowning with Thorns, c. 1602–1604 or 1607
Caravaggio (1573–1610)

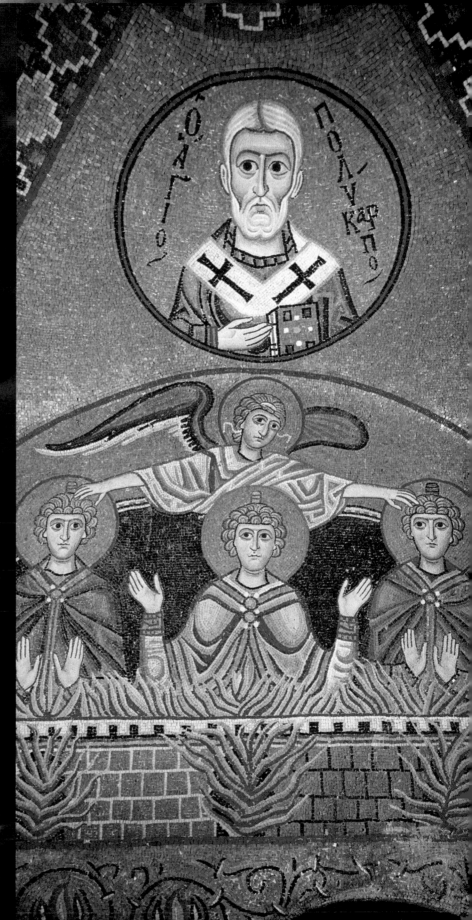

he commanded some of his strongest soldiers to tie up the men and throw them into the flaming furnace. The king wanted it done at that very moment. So the soldiers tied up Shadrach, Meshach, and Abednego and threw them into the flaming furnace with all of their clothes still on, including their turbans. The fire was so hot that flames leaped out and killed the soldiers.

Suddenly the king jumped up and shouted, "Weren't only three men tied up and thrown into the fire?"

"Yes, Your Majesty," his officers answered.

"But I see four men walking around in the fire," the king replied. "None of them is tied up or harmed, and the fourth one looks like a god." Nebuchadnezzar went closer to the flaming furnace and said to the three young men, "You servants of the Most High God, come out at once!"

They came out, and the king's high officials, governors, and advisors all crowded around them. The men were not burned, their hair wasn't scorched, and their clothes didn't even smell like smoke. King Nebuchadnezzar said:

"Praise their God for sending an angel to rescue his servants! They trusted their God and refused to obey my commands. Yes, they chose to die rather than to worship or serve any god except their own. And I won't allow people of any nation or race to say anything against their God. Anyone who does will be chopped up and their houses will be torn down, because no other god has such great power to save."

above: Detail of the Ishtar Gate

Shadrach, Meshach, and Abednego, the Three Youths in the Fiery Furnace of Nebuchadnezzar 11th-century Byzantine mosaic, monastery of Hosios Loukas, Greece

45

First-Century Prison Breaks

The life of a first-century apostle was full of risk. The book of Acts records three instances when one or more of the apostles was imprisoned, only to miraculously escape.

The circumstances surrounding these escapes grow more bizarre and mysterious with each occurrence. The first account is found in Acts 5:17–25. Much like Jesus, the apostles performed many miraculous acts of healing. Needless to say, these events attracted large crowds, and the high priest and the Jewish ruling council envied the attention. As a result, they had Peter and the others thrown in jail.

This imprisonment didn't last long, however; during the night, an angel freed the apostles. When the high priest sent for them the next day, the jailers found the jail locked and the guards in place, but the cell was empty. The apostles were discovered preaching in the temple.

As the first century progressed, local persecution against Christians grew more intense, particularly during the reign of King Herod Agrippa. He had James, one of the disciples who was also the brother of the apostle John, beheaded. Herod's persecution pleased the Jewish leaders, who saw the early followers of Christ as heretics who had abandoned their Jewish heritage. Eventually, persecution forced those Christians to scatter away from Jerusalem and relocate throughout the region.

During Herod's reign, Peter returned to Jerusalem to meet with the remaining members of the church there. But Herod had Peter thrown in jail and assigned not one but four squads of soldiers to watch him (Acts 12:1–4). The night before Peter's trial was to begin, an angel appeared in his cell, woke him, and released him from his chains. No explanation was given, just the command to get up and go. After leading Peter from his cell and past the prison gates that mysteriously opened by themselves, the angel disappeared without warning. Peter made his way to the house of Mary, John's mother, where he shared his incredible story with the believers who had gathered there to pray for him.

The third and most unusual prison break is found in Acts 16:16–39. During Paul's second missionary journey, he and his colleague Silas were in Philippi where they met a young girl who was in double bondage. She was possessed by a demon and owned as a slave. Her owner made money by having her tell the future, a mysterious power that the author of Acts saw as something made possible by the demonic spirit that controlled her.

READ IT FOR YOURSELF

ACTS 5:17–25

The high priest and all the other Sadducees who were with him became jealous. They arrested the apostles and put them in the city jail. But that night an angel from the Lord opened the doors of the jail and led the apostles out. The angel said, "Go to the temple and tell the people everything about this new life." So they went into the temple before sunrise and started teaching.

The high priest and his men called together their council, which included all of Israel's leaders. Then they ordered the apostles to be brought to them from the jail. The temple police who were sent to the jail did not find the apostles. They returned and said, "We found the jail locked tight and the guards standing at the doors. But when we opened the doors and went in, we didn't find anyone there." The captain of the temple police and the chief priests listened to their report, but they did not know what to think about it.

Just then someone came in and said, "Now those men you put in jail are in the temple, teaching the people!"

Mamertine Prison, Forum Romanum, Rome, Italy
This is the jail where Saint Peter may have been imprisoned.

Liberation of St. Peter
Bartolomé Esteban Murillo (1617–1682)

were preaching. Exasperated, Paul ordered the demon to leave her body, and it did. This of course infuriated her owners, because not only had the evil spirit departed from her, but the owners could no longer profit from her ability to reveal the future. Her owners lodged a complaint with the city officials, charging that Paul and Silas were disturbing the peace. The two missionaries were beaten and thrown in jail, locked in chains, and put under a guard's watch.

At midnight, as the two men prayed and sang while the other prisoners listened, an earthquake shook the jail. The tremor was so violent that the doors burst open. Even more bizarre, the chains fell from all the prisoners, suggesting this was no ordinary earthquake.

The jailer was, of course, alarmed, thinking the prisoners had all escaped under his watch. Doubtless he would pay with his life for such failure of duty. As the jailer prepared to kill himself rather than face certain execution, Paul stopped him. Unfathomably, none of the prisoners had left.

Instead of escaping into the night, Paul and Silas met with the jailer and his family—all of whom came to believe in Paul's message. Paul and Silas returned to the jail that night, but they were released the following morning.

A Reading from Acts 12:6–11

The night before Peter was to be put on trial, he was asleep and bound by two chains. A soldier was guarding him on each side, and two other soldiers were guarding the entrance to the jail. Suddenly an angel from the Lord appeared, and light flashed around in the cell. The angel poked Peter in the side and woke him up. Then he said, "Quick! Get up!"

The chains fell off his hands, and the angel said, "Get dressed and put on your sandals." Peter did what he was told. Then the angel said, "Now put on your coat and follow me." Peter left with the angel, but he thought everything was only a dream. They went past the two groups of soldiers, and when they came to the iron gate to the city, it opened by itself. They went out and were going along the street, when all at once the angel disappeared.

Peter now realized what had happened, and he said, "I am certain that the Lord sent his angel to rescue me from Herod and from everything the Jewish leaders planned to do to me."

Life from Death

Saint Peter
6th-century encaustic icon from Saint Catherine's Monastery, Mount Sinai

Bringing the dead back to life is surely the most astounding act of deliverance. On more than one occasion, the apostles Peter and Paul did just that.

Acts 9 tells of a woman named Dorcas, also known as Tabitha, who lived in Joppa. She had a reputation for doing good deeds and giving to the poor. When Dorcas died, her friends sent for Peter, a disciple of Jesus who had a reputation for performing miraculous healings. When Peter saw Dorcas's lifeless body, he prayed. Then he simply commanded her to get up. Just like that, according to the biblical account, she opened her eyes and sat up.

Some time later, as Paul was in the midst of his final missionary journey, he was preparing to say good-bye to the Christian believers in Troas. On his final night there, he gathered a group together and addressed them well into the late hours of the night. While listening to Paul, a young man named Eutychus—who was perched precariously on a window sill—went to sleep and fell out of the window, dropping three floors to the ground.

Eutychus was dead by the time Paul got to him. However, seemingly within minutes, Paul announced to the worried assembly that Eutychus had returned to life. Readers of Acts are left to wonder how Paul performed this remarkable healing. (Read the full account in Acts 20:7–12.)

A Reading from Acts 9:36–43

In Joppa there was a follower named Tabitha. Her Greek name was Dorcas, which means "deer." She was always doing good things for people and had given much to the poor. But she got sick and died, and her body was washed and placed in an upstairs room. Joppa wasn't far from Lydda, and the followers heard that Peter was there. They sent two men to say to him, "Please come with us as quickly as you can!" At once, Peter went with them.

The men took Peter upstairs into the room. Many widows were there crying. They showed him the coats and clothes that Dorcas had made while she was still alive.

After Peter had sent everyone out of the room, he knelt down and prayed. Then he turned to the body of Dorcas and said, "Tabitha, get up!" The woman opened her eyes, and when she saw Peter, she sat up. He took her by the hand and helped her to her feet.

Peter called in the widows and the other followers and showed them that Dorcas had been raised from death. Everyone in Joppa heard what had happened, and many of them put their faith in the Lord. Peter stayed on for a while in Joppa in the house of a man named Simon, who made leather.

Raising of Tabitha
Masolino Da Panicale (1383–1447)

Reluctant Prophet, Unlikely Audience

It's a whale of a tale. When God called on Jonah to preach to residents of an enemy city, Jonah chose to run rather than obey. When Jonah tried to escape, God arranged special accommodations for the reluctant prophet: inside the belly of a large fish.

Whale Swallows Jonah
Ethiopian folk art, 20th century

Jonah was called by God to warn the people of Nineveh that their city would be destroyed because of their evil ways. The basic details of Jonah's story are known to many—namely, his attempt to refuse God's call, resulting in an unpleasant man-overboard-swallowed-by-large-fish experience.

Jonah didn't hesitate. He boarded a boat going the other way. He ended up being thrown overboard, at which point God sent a large fish to swallow him. Jonah somehow survived for three days before being vomited onto the shore.

Reluctantly, Jonah journeyed to Nineveh in the end, and surprisingly, the city repented of its ways. But it was a short-lived contrition. Two other prophets, Nahum and Zephaniah, later predicted the downfall of Assyria's capital.

IN THE BELLY OF THE EARTH

Jesus made a cryptic reference to Jonah during one of his many confrontations with his opponents. Just as Jonah spent three days in the belly of a fish, Jesus said, so he would spend three days in the belly of the earth—a veiled reference to his death and resurrection (Matthew 12:38–42).

Christ Glorified in the Court of Heaven
Fra Angelico (Guido di Pietro) (c.1387–1455)

CHAPTER 5

Heavenly Secrets: The World of Angels

When reading the Bible, you're bound to come across an angel or two at some point. But who are these strange celestial beings?

The biblical term that we translate as *angel* means "messenger," an indication of their primary role. Throughout Scripture, angels were often sent to announce God's plans—such as the enigmatic visitors who appeared to Abraham and predicted the birth of his son Isaac (Genesis 18:1–15), the multitude of angels who announced Jesus' birth (Luke 2:8–15), or the *"young man in a white robe"* who met some of Jesus' followers after his resurrection (Mark 16:1–8).

What do angels look like? The Bible offers few clues to this puzzle. Often angels appear in human form, indistinguishable from regular people. Apart from a few sparse descriptions, like those found in Genesis 19:1–2 and Mark 16:5, we know very little about the appearance of angels—making them even more mysterious.

One thing we do know: not all angels are good. Some rebel against God, choosing to work in opposition to him.

What role do angels play in our lives today—for good or bad?

Gloria in excelsis deo et in terra

The Annunciation to the Shepherds
Boucicaut Master n.d. (1405–1408)

Divine Instruments:
Mediating the Mysteries of God

From time to time, the Bible depicts angels entering into the human story, revealing the secret purposes of God, mediating the divine presence, and announcing epoch-shifting events.

Most often, this meant serving as a sort of divine messenger—someone entrusted with God's secrets, not to keep them hidden but to reveal them to his people. For example, an angel once appeared to a group of shepherds outside Bethlehem, announcing the birth of Jesus (Luke 2:10–11). This would not be the last momentous event to be heralded by angels, either. According to Luke 24:6, two angels delivered news of Jesus' resurrection to the women at the tomb: *"Jesus isn't here! He has been raised from death."* (You can read the full account of Jesus' resurrection in Luke 24:1–35.)

Sometimes the message the angels delivered was one of encouragement, and sometimes that encouragement took the form of more than just words. Whether it was protecting three young men inside a fiery furnace (Daniel 3) or rescuing the apostles from prison (Acts 5:19), angels occasionally served as God's instrument of protection for his people. According to the writer of Hebrews, angels serve those *"who are going to be saved"* (1:14).

In the Bible, angels provide not only physical protection and support but spiritual strength and encouragement as well.

Both Matthew and Mark say that angels came to help Jesus when he was in the desert for forty days (Matthew 4:11; Mark 1:13). Luke's Gospel reports that an angel appeared to Jesus as he prayed for strength to yield to God's will that he suffer and die (Luke 22:43).

However, angelic labors were not always positive and encouraging. There were times when God's emissaries enacted divine judgment on the wickedness of the world. For example, Genesis 19 describes the fate of the corrupt towns of Sodom and Gomorrah, when two angels appeared at Lot's home in Sodom to warn him of the coming destruction. It was also an angel who struck down King Herod Agrippa for trying to steal honor that belonged only to God (Acts 12:23). And the book of Revelation includes several cryptic scenes in which angels serve as instruments of God's judgment on the wicked (Revelation 8:6–9:21 and 16:1–17).

In each of these angelic appearances, the overarching purposes of God are revealed through his angels. They mediate the invisible and make known the unknowable; they are emissaries of God's divine presence and will. They are God's instrument of mercy and justice, even when his judgment is stern.

Abraham and the Three Angels
James Tissot (1836–1902)

A Reading from
Matthew 26:51–53

One of Jesus' followers pulled out a sword. He struck the servant of the high priest and cut off his ear.

But Jesus told him, "Put your sword away. Anyone who lives by fighting will die by fighting. Don't you know that I could ask my Father, and he would at once send me more than twelve armies of angels?"

Angels Demystified:
Some Common Misunderstandings Explained

Because the Bible reveals relatively little about the nature of celestial beings, a number of traditions and legends regarding angels have developed that are not supported by Scripture.

MISUNDERSTANDINGS:

ANGELS WERE NOT CREATED BY GOD

What the Bible Says: Perhaps this idea came from the fact that angels are mysteriously absent from the biblical accounts of creation (Genesis 1–2). In the New Testament, however, the Bible clears up any uncertainty about the origin of angels. In Colossians 1:15–16, Paul confirms that angels were created by God:

Christ is exactly like God,
who cannot be seen.
He is the first-born Son,
superior to all creation.

Everything was created by him,
everything in heaven
and on earth,
everything seen and unseen,
including all forces
and powers,
and all rulers
and authorities.
All things were created
by God's Son,
and everything was made
for him.

ANGELS ARE MATERIAL BEINGS

What the Bible Says: As noted earlier, the Bible records a number of episodes in which angels appear in human form, but these instances are temporary manifestations of a spiritual being in physical form. In one of the more bizarre scenes in the Bible, for example, Jacob wrestles an angel (Genesis 32); the patriarch's hip is dislocated in the process. And in Genesis 18, three men appear unannounced to Abraham and Sarah to announce that a son will be born to them. Elsewhere the biblical authors seem to understand angels as immaterial creatures without physical bodies. The writer of Hebrews calls them *"spirits"* (1:14). Paul refers to fallen angels as *"rulers of darkness and powers in the spiritual world"* (Ephesians 6:12). Both Matthew and Luke (the author of Acts) identify demons (another name for fallen angels) as *"evil spirits"* (Matthew 8:16; Acts 19:12). The apparent lack of a material body is a key element that sets these celestial beings apart from humans.

ANGELS ARE DIVINE

What the Bible Says: The longest passage about angels (Hebrews 1–2) reveals that these strange beings are superior to humans but inferior to Christ. The author of Hebrews states that God's Son was also a messenger (1:2), but because of the special Father/Son relationship between God and Jesus (1:5), Jesus is superior to any angel. Therefore, angels are commanded by God to worship God's Son (1:6). In the biblical narrative, angels act strictly as God's servants, carrying out his plans and delivering messages on God's behalf. Angels do have free will, and those in heaven choose to obey God (Matthew 6:10), while those who chose to rebel have been cast into a dark pit until the day of judgment (2 Peter 2:4; Jude 6), when they will be sent into an everlasting fire (Matthew 25:41). God alone is infinite and has the power to create and destroy.

Given that angels are not infinite, it is not surprising to discover they are not all-knowing, all-powerful, or present everywhere.

ANGELS ARE DEAD OR GLORIFIED HUMANS

The Bible reserves such characteristics for God alone. While angels seem to have access to knowledge surpassing our own (see, for example, Galatians 3:19), their knowledge does have limits (Matthew 24:36; Luke 12:8). Angels are subject to the power of God, and they serve as agents of his will (Psalm 103:20).

Many students of the Bible believe that Satan himself is a fallen angel. His power is limited—as can be seen in his confrontation with God in the book of Job and his ultimate fate as described in Revelation.

What the Bible Says: Perhaps one of the most popular ideas about angels is that they are dead humans who have been glorified by God in some special way. Some people take comfort in the belief that their deceased relatives watch over them from heaven. However, the Bible does not equate angels with humans who have died. As noted previously, angels do not seem to be material beings with physical bodies.

READ IT FOR YOURSELF

LUKE 20:35–36

But in the future world no one who is worthy to rise from death will either marry or die. They will be like the angels and will be God's children, because they have been raised to life.

HEBREWS 1:6–8a

When God brings his first-born Son into the world, he commands all of his angels to worship him. And when God speaks about the angels, he says, "I change my angels into wind and my servants into flaming fire." But God says about his Son, "You are God, and you will rule as King forever!"

Fallen Angels

If we think we know little about God's angels and their work in the world, we know even less about their fallen counterparts.

A Reading from Luke 10:17–20

When the 72 followers returned, they were excited and said, "Lord, even the demons obeyed when we spoke in your name!"

Jesus told them: "I saw Satan fall from heaven like a flash of lightning. I have given you the power to trample on snakes and scorpions and to defeat the power of your enemy Satan. Nothing can harm you. But don't be happy because evil spirits obey you. Be happy that your names are written in heaven!"

Typically included in this category are demons and the apparent head of all demonic powers, Satan (also known as the devil). But how did fallen angels become fallen, and what is their work in the world? These are questions on which Scripture is fairly silent. But the biblical narrative seems to offer a few tantalizing clues to this mystery.

Many biblical scholars agree that fallen angels were originally good, like everything else God created. However, they rebelled against God and became evil and were cast out of heaven (away from God's presence), resulting in their "fallen" state. This understanding is based primarily on two New Testament passages that refer to angels who *"sinned"* and *"left their proper places"* (2 Peter 2:4; Jude 6). The author of 2 Peter went on to compare the state of the fallen angels to the state of wicked humans who will eventually be subject to judgment (see also John 12:31).

Satan, who is sometimes seen as the head of the fallen angels, seems to be a demon himself (see Matthew 12:24, 27 and Luke 10:17–20). In the Hebrew language of the Old Testament, the name Satan is a form of a verb that means "to act as an adversary." Several other terms used for Satan expose other dark aspects of his character: tempter, enemy, evil one, father of lies, great dragon, and deceiver, to name a few. For examples of his deceptive nature, see such passages as Genesis 3, 2 Corinthians 11:14–15, 1 Thessalonians 2:18, and Revelation 12:9, along with the Gospel accounts of the temptation of Jesus (Matthew 4:1–11; Mark 1:12–13; Luke 4:1–13), the parable of the weeds (Matthew 13:24–30, 36–43), or Judas's betrayal of Jesus (John 13:21–30).

For their part, the demons seem to follow Satan's lead, occupying themselves with tempting and deceiving people—all in an effort to keep them alienated from God. In some passages of Scripture, the "mischief" seems to include causing both mental and physical torment (see Matthew 12:22; Mark 9:17; Acts 8:7; Ephesians 6:12).

As intimidating a prospect as demonic possession may be, the Bible reveals that all is not lost against Satan and the demons; God's power trumps the power of evil. The book of Job, for example, hints at the limited nature of Satan's power, in contrast to God's. The author of the letter of James promises believers that if they resist the devil, *"he will run from you"* (4:7). We can also take heart that Scripture points toward a final outcome in which good wins and evil is destroyed forever.

URIEL: FIRE OF GOD

The book of 2 Esdras, also called Apocalypse of Esdras, is included in the Apocrypha, a group of early Jewish writings that is sometimes included with the Christian Bible. The book is made up of seven visions, the first of which includes an angel named Uriel. As Esdras laments his people's affliction, Uriel informs him that the past is longer than the future will be. The rest of the visions regard the end of the age.

Uriel, whose name means "light or fire of God," also appears in the book of 1 Enoch (another apocryphal writing). In this book, Uriel teaches Enoch the secrets of the sun and is identified as the angel that spoke of the coming deluge (1 Enoch 72–83).

Though a lesser-known angel than Gabriel or Michael, Uriel also appears in Milton's *Paradise Lost* and Haydn's oratorio, *The Creation*.

Detail of *The Triumph of St. Augustine*
Claudio Coello (c. 1642–1693)

Spiritual Warfare:
Invisible Battle of Good vs. Evil

A Reading from Matthew 4:1–11

The Holy Spirit led Jesus into the desert, so that the devil could test him. After Jesus had gone without eating for 40 days and nights, he was very hungry. Then the devil came to him and said, "If you are God's Son, tell these stones to turn into bread."

Jesus answered, "The Scriptures say: 'No one can live only on food. People need every word that God has spoken.'"

Next, the devil took Jesus into the holy city to the highest part of the temple. The devil said, "If you are God's Son, jump off. The Scriptures say: 'God will give his angels orders about you. They will catch you in their arms, and you won't hurt your feet on the stones.'"

Jesus answered, "The Scriptures also say, 'Don't try to test the Lord your God!'"

Finally, the devil took Jesus up on a very high mountain and showed him all the kingdoms on earth and their power. The devil said to him, "I will give all this to you, if you will bow down and worship me."

Jesus answered, "Go away Satan! The Scriptures say: 'Worship the Lord your God and serve only him.'"

Then the devil left Jesus, and angels came to help him.

Him the Almighty Power Hurled Headlong Flaming from the Eternal Sky
Gustave Doré (1832–1883)

The idea that there is some kind of invisible, spiritual war going on around us can be difficult to fathom. Nevertheless, the Bible hints that such a conflict began with the fall of the angels (Luke 10:18). Although victory was made certain by Christ's resurrection, ultimate success will not be achieved until evil is punished once and for all at a time known only to God.

An example of spiritual warfare can be seen in the temptation of Jesus (Matthew 4:1–11). According to Matthew, Mark, and Luke, Satan tried to entice Jesus to test God. The tempter even quoted Scripture in an effort to convince Jesus to worship him instead of God, but Jesus refused. After Satan left, angels appeared to assist Jesus, who had been weakened by his forty-day fast in the desert. Many see a hidden meaning to the battle in the desert wilderness, regarding it as a foreshadowing of Jesus' road to the cross, where he would be tempted by Satan once more to abandon the work God had sent him to do (Hebrews 2:14–18).

There were also a number of incidents when Jesus encountered people who were regarded as demon possessed. Though the precise nature of demon possession remains a mystery, the interactions between Jesus and the demons provide some useful insight into spiritual conflict. According to Luke's Gospel, when Jesus encountered a man possessed by several demons, they begged Jesus not to torture them. So instead, Jesus cast them into a herd of pigs nearby (Luke 8:26–36). This is just one of many instances in the New Testament in which Jesus publicly confronted and defeated demons who were wreaking havoc in people's lives.

The mind-boggling visions captured in the book of Revelation describe a final, cataclysmic battle between good and evil, resulting in the ultimate defeat of all that is evil. Revelation 12 describes war breaking out in heaven; the archangel Michael and his mighty army of angels take arms against a dragon and those loyal to it (Revelation 12:7). The enemies of God are thrown from heaven to earth. In anger, the dragon wages war against those who are faithful to God (Revelation 17).

Michael Defeating the Fallen Angels, 1660–1665
Luca Giordano

At the end of the battle, however, the great deceiver—*"the devil who fooled them"*—is thrown permanently into a burning lake (Revelation 20:10).

Icon of the archangel Michael
Egyptian School (18th century)

Angelic Identities Revealed

Their appearances in the Bible are fleeting and often shrouded in mystery. They have the ability to inspire awe and terror, hope and fear. Yet within the Protestant canon we meet only a handful of individual angels—and only two (not counting the fallen angel Satan) are introduced by name: Gabriel and Michael. Still, these powerful spiritual beings often play an important role in the biblical story.

Michael is identified by the New Testament as an "archangel," a term meaning "chief angel." Whether he is the only archangel remains a mystery, but he is the only one so named in the Bible.

Michael always seems ready for a fight. The book of Daniel, which describes him as *"one of the strongest guardian angels,"* mentions a hostile encounter between Michael and the prince (or "guardian angel") of Persia (Daniel 10). In the New Testament, Jude's tiny letter contains a cryptic reference to an argument between Michael and Satan over the body of Moses (Jude 9).

Gabriel is mentioned four times in the Bible—each time delivering a vital message. He appeared twice to the prophet Daniel (8:17; 9:20–21), then reappeared in the New Testament, when he announced the birth of Jesus' cousin and Jesus himself (Luke 1:5–38). Some speculate that Gabriel is also an archangel because he, like Michael, is identified by name. However, the Bible is silent on this question; we are left to ponder the secret of Gabriel's identity.

Even those angels whose names remain a secret are beings of awesome power, capable of instilling a mystifying sense of foreboding. For example, the Bible mentions a destroying angel—or the angel of death—who carries out God's judgment on the world.

Seraphim make perhaps only two appearances in the Bible, but each time it is clear that they play an important role in God's order. The term is derived from the Hebrew word *seraph*, which, when used as a verb, means "to burn." When used as a noun, it means "a fiery, flying serpent." This somewhat terrifying image seems to suggest a kind of angelic creature that takes the form of a winged serpent such as the flaming creatures that appeared in Isaiah's vision (Isaiah 6:2).

The cherubim are sometimes understood to be a relatively lower class of beings. Some versions of the Bible (including the CEV) refer to cherubim as *"winged creatures,"* perhaps because that is the physical characteristic most often associated with this type of angelic being. One description of cherubim can be found in Exodus 25:18–20; images of these winged creatures were fashioned out of gold and adorned the sacred chest (ark of the covenant).

HEAVENLY WARRIOR

Gabriel, 1991
Laura James

The name Gabriel means "God is my warrior."

READ IT FOR YOURSELF

JUDE 9

Even Michael, the chief angel, didn't dare to insult the devil, when the two of them were arguing about the body of Moses. All Michael said was, "The Lord will punish you!"

Angel of Death:
Shadowy Destroyer

The term "destroying angel"—alternatively known as the "angel that brings death" (Exodus 12:23)—seems straightforward enough. The name says it all. In reality, however, little is known about the destroying angel. What can be discerned centers on three passages of Scripture. Nowhere is the destroying angel named. We do not even know whether these three passages refer to the same angel or simply describe a task that any angel can perform. Alarmingly enough, Psalm 78:49 alludes to "swarms of destroying angels."

The first mention of a destroying angel is in Exodus 12. The great leader Moses is in the midst of his legendary confrontation with Pharaoh, the king of Egypt, trying to persuade the stubborn ruler to release the Israelites from slavery in Egypt. Nine devastating plagues had failed to soften Pharaoh's heart, but for the final plague, God sent the *"angel that brings death"* to kill the firstborn son of every Egyptian family (12:23). This same angel spared—or passed over—the firstborn sons of the Israelite families.

The next time a destroying angel appears in Scripture is during the reign of King David (2 Samuel 24:1–17). In his pride David took a census to count how many fighting men were in his army. As punishment for David's conceit, God sent a destroying angel to afflict the nation with a debilitating disease—perhaps meant to serve as a painful reminder of the nation's fragility. Soon, however, God took pity on the people and stopped the mission.

The third appearance of a destroying angel is in 2 Kings 19. At the time, Hezekiah was king of Judah, and the capital city of Jerusalem was under siege by King Sennacherib and the Assyrian army. When Hezekiah cried out for deliverance, God sent a destroying angel to the Assyrian camp, and the angel killed 185,000 men (2 Kings 19:35).

A destroying angel brought death. While this angel—or group of angels—remains shrouded in mystery, the very notion of a destroying angel provided a sobering reminder that God is sovereign over the events of the world.

READ IT FOR YOURSELF

HEBREWS 11:27–28

Because of his faith, Moses left Egypt. Moses had seen the invisible God and wasn't afraid of the king's anger. His faith also made him celebrate Passover. He sprinkled the blood of animals on the doorposts, so that the first-born sons of the people of Israel would not be killed by the destroying angel.

THE ANGEL OF DEATH

And Then There was a Great Cry in Egypt, Arthur Hacker (1858–1919)

The Firstborn Slain, Gustave Doré (1832–1883)

A Reading from Exodus 12:29–31

At midnight the LORD killed the first-born son of every Egyptian family, from the son of the king to the son of every prisoner in jail. He also killed the first-born male of every animal that belonged to the Egyptians.

That night the king, his officials, and everyone else in Egypt got up and started crying bitterly. In every Egyptian home, someone was dead.

During the night the king sent for Moses and Aaron and told them, "Get your people out of my country and leave us alone! Go and worship the LORD, as you have asked."

63

CHAPTER 6

Strange Tales: Foretold and Fulfilled

Warriors and kings took center stage in Israel's story; to them belonged the glory and spoils of war. Yet among Israel's leaders, none were more greatly feared—or misunderstood—than the prophets.

Even today, misconceptions abound about these enigmatic figures from Israel's past. Prophets are commonly thought to have forecasted the future. More often, though, prophets encouraged, reprimanded, and shared God's message with anyone who would listen. They urged people to return to God, to have compassion on the poor, and to demonstrate God's love to all people.

Prophets' methods ranged from the conventional to the bizarre. Some communicated through dramatic public acts, like shaving their heads or calling down fire from heaven. Their messages featured themes of unimaginable judgment and unwavering hope, sometimes in practically the same breath.

Many in the ancient world clung to prophetic oracles, hoping to uncover a message from God—some insight into his will and his plans for the future.

Who were these mysterious prophets, and what did they reveal about the divine mystery?

The Prophets:
Decoded

WHO'S WHO

Seventeen of the Old Testament books are considered prophetic, though many of the historical writings contain sections of prophecy as well.

MAJOR PROPHETS

ISAIAH
JEREMIAH
LAMENTATIONS*
EZEKIEL
DANIEL**

MINOR PROPHETS†

HOSEA
JOEL
AMOS
OBADIAH
JONAH
MICAH
NAHUM
HABAKKUK
ZEPHANIAH
HAGGAI
ZECHARIAH
MALACHI

*The book of Lamentations is a collection of poems lamenting the destruction of Jerusalem in 586 BC.

**The book of Daniel is technically an apocalypse, though Daniel the individual is regarded as one of the prophets.

† This name refers to the relatively short length of these books, not their significance. The twelve Minor Prophets could easily fit on a single scroll.

The Test of a True Prophet

Not everyone who claimed the prophet's mantle was worthy of it. In his farewell address, Moses, Israel's chief lawgiver, defined the role of a prophet—and gave a simple test for distinguishing false prophets from the real thing:

Moses said to Israel:

You were asking for a prophet the day you were gathered at Mount Sinai and said to the LORD, "Please don't let us hear your voice or see this terrible fire again—if we do, we will die!" Then the LORD told me:

Moses, they have said the right thing. So when I want to speak to them, I will choose one of them to be a prophet like you. I will give my message to that prophet, who will tell the people exactly what I have said. Since the message comes from me, anyone who doesn't obey the message will have to answer to me. . . .

Moses said to Israel:

You may be asking yourselves, "How can we tell if a prophet's message really comes from the LORD?" You will know, because if the LORD says something will happen, it will happen. And if it doesn't, you will know that the prophet was falsely claiming to speak for the LORD. Don't be afraid of any prophet whose message doesn't come from the LORD.

Deuteronomy 18:16–22

OUTSIDERS ON THE INSIDE

Prophets played an important role in every chapter of Israel's development. At times, they simply communicated God's truth to people, reminding them not to worship idols or admonishing them to care for the poor. At other times, prophets warned the people of coming judgment.

Serving as the nation's conscience often drove a wedge between prophets and their fellow Israelites. While some prophets functioned as royal advisers, others stood on the fringes of society, protesting an often-corrupt establishment from the outside.

A prophet was a privileged gatekeeper of heavenly secrets, yet such a responsibility carried the risk of alienation, derision, and persecution.

NOT CRYSTAL BALLS AND TEA LEAVES

BIBLICAL PROPHECY BEARS LITTLE RESEMBLANCE TO ASTROLOGY OR FORTUNE-TELLING, NOR IS IT MERELY AN ATTEMPT TO DIVINE THE FUTURE.

In our modern world, shaped by technology and founded on empirical evidence, the role of a prophet may seem fantastical, even mystical. However, there is much more to biblical prophecy than foretelling the future. The prophet's main objective was spiritual: to inspire people to put their trust in God. The role of a prophet was not necessarily to unlock every secret of the future. Indeed, the most famous biblical prophecies don't just reveal events ahead of time; they remind us of God's control over these mysterious events.

The prophecies of the Bible always reveal something about God's plan for the world. Many Old Testament prophecies described God's judgment and restoration of his people. As understood by Christians, the prophecies concerning a suffering servant and savior point to Jesus as the promised Messiah. Apocalyptic literature about the end of human history reminds readers of the final judgment and kindles hope in anticipation of God's new creation.

READ IT FOR YOURSELF

DEUTERONOMY 18:9–12

Soon you will go into the land that the LORD your God is giving you. The nations that live there do things that are disgusting to the LORD, and you must not follow their example. Don't sacrifice your son or daughter. And don't try to use any kind of magic or witchcraft to tell fortunes or to cast spells or to talk with spirits of the dead. The LORD is disgusted with anyone who does these things, and that's why he will help you destroy the nations that are in the land.

PURPOSE OF PROPHECY

Prophecy can inspire and inform us to live each day with confident anticipation as God's revelations continue to unfold. Lives can change when people trust that God's plan is in place and that they have been empowered to be enjoined to God's mission in carrying out that plan. In the end, that is the central, redeeming message behind the prophecies of the Bible.

The Promise to Abraham

In the first book of the Bible, God spoke to a man from Ur in Chaldea named Abram (later renamed Abraham, meaning "father of many"). Abram was so moved by this divine encounter that he packed up his family and left the home of his ancestors in Ur near the Persian Gulf, heeding God's instructions to go to the unfamiliar land of Canaan.

What prompted Abraham to make such an unlikely move? Nothing less than an impossible prophecy with lasting repercussions. God promised to bless Abraham beyond his wildest dreams: *"I will bless you and make your descendants into a great nation. You will become famous and be a blessing to others. I will bless those who bless you, but I will put a curse on anyone who puts a curse on you. Everyone on earth will be blessed because of you"* (Genesis 12:2–3).

Yet there was a seemingly impossible paradox in God's promise. In order to be the "father of many," one must have children—but Abraham and his wife Sarah were unable to conceive. Fulfilling this prophecy would require a miracle of incomprehensible magnitude.

"I WILL BLESS YOU AND MAKE YOUR DESCENDANTS INTO A GREAT NATION. YOU WILL BECOME FAMOUS AND BE A BLESSING TO OTHERS. I WILL BLESS THOSE WHO BLESS YOU, BUT I WILL PUT A CURSE ON ANYONE WHO PUTS A CURSE ON YOU. EVERYONE ON EARTH WILL BE BLESSED BECAUSE OF YOU."

GENESIS 12:2–3

Isaac: Mystery Child

God's promise to Abraham seemed to hit a dead end—namely, that Abraham and Sarah remained childless. But, God reiterated the promise given years before, making it clear that Sarah was to bear Abraham's child: "I will bless [Sarah], and you will have a son by her" (Genesis 17:16a).

Because Abraham and Sarah were quite old when God promised them a child, they could not imagine the prophecy coming true. So they devised their own solution to the mystery of how Abraham's descendants would become a *"great nation."* Sarah suggested that Abraham have a baby with her servant Hagar (Genesis 16), who would act as a surrogate mother for her. When the child was born, he was named Ishmael.

Though this practice was culturally acceptable at the time, God had other plans for Abraham's offspring. Eventually, Sarah became pregnant and gave birth to Isaac, just as God had promised. Later Isaac became the father of Jacob, whose twelve sons became the heads of the twelve tribes that came to be known as Israel. This was the fulfillment of God's promise to Abraham (Genesis 35:23–26).

However, the promise to Abraham had a deeper, hidden meaning as well. God had promised that *"everyone on earth"* would be blessed because of Abraham's descendants. Centuries later, Christian writers would connect this prophecy to Jesus, a descendant of Abraham whose death and resurrection brought salvation to the entire world. The apostle Paul, author of several New Testament books, wrote that *"everyone who has faith is a child of Abraham"* (Galatians 3:7).

READ IT FOR YOURSELF

GENESIS 17:6–7

"I will give you a lot of descendants, and they will become great nations. Some of them will even be kings. I will always keep the promise I have made to you and your descendants, because I am your God and their God."

Abraham Sends Hagar Away, 1837
Horace Vernet (1789–1863)

The Strange Collapse of Egypt

Egypt looms large in Israel's history. As a neighbor to the southwest on the fertile banks of the Nile River, Egypt often played a role in the development of Israel. Abraham and his grandson Jacob both took refuge in Egypt during times of famine. Joseph, one of Jacob's sons, was even appointed by the king of Egypt to serve as a governor. It was also in Egypt that Jacob's descendants grew into the nation of Israel, and from Egypt that they fled in the Exodus. Centuries later, Jesus, Mary, and Joseph escaped the murderous Herod the Great by finding refuge in Egypt.

Egypt was a world power from 4300 BC until about 600 BC—often wielding its might and influence over Israel. The prophets Ezekiel and Jeremiah spoke of Egypt's eventual fall from power (Jeremiah 46; Ezekiel 29–32). Ezekiel wrote that Egypt would recover from desolation (perhaps a reference to an attack by the Babylonians), but that it would never again rule as widely (Ezekiel 29:13–15).

How exactly these prophecies relate to history remains a mystery. Over time, Egypt faced many defeats, yet with each one it reestablished itself as a nation. Ezekiel's prophecy may have been fulfilled in that Egypt no longer reached beyond its own borders the way it had in the past.

Egypt

POINT OF INTEREST

The pyramids of Egypt are some of the most mysterious structures on earth. Some have speculated they were built by Hebrew slaves; however, the pyramids predate Israel's enslavement in Egypt. According to the Bible, the Hebrews were forced to build the Egyptian cities of Pithom and Rameses (Exodus 1:11).

Egypt is famous for its ancient civilization and some of the world's most well-known monuments including the Giza pyramid complex and its Great Sphinx. The southern city of Luxor contains numerous ancient artifacts such as the Karnak Temple and the Valley of the Kings. Egypt is widely regarded as an important political and cultural nation of the Middle East.

Capital	Cairo
Language	Arabic
Ethnic Groups	
	98% Egyptian
	1% Nubian
	1% European
First Dynasty	c. 3150 BC

The city of Cairo

Mysterious Message:
The Curse of Jericho

Joshua's battle against Jericho is one of the best-known (not to mention most unorthodox) military battles of the Bible. As the story goes, God himself devised the winning strategy: March around the city—once a day, every day for six days—but seven times on the seventh day. Then, everybody shout!

According to Joshua 6, this mystifying strategy brought Jericho's protective walls crashing down. What once had been a formidable fortress suddenly became a pile of stones—easy pickings.

Following Jericho's defeat, the Israelite commander prophesied a strange curse against anyone who might try to rebuild the city. According to Joshua's curse, that man's oldest son would die the moment he began laying the foundation, and the rest of his children would perish by the time the city gates were finished (Joshua 6:26).

A few centuries later, someone did rebuild Jericho. His unfortunate story is recorded in the book of 1 Kings:

"While Ahab was king, a man from Bethel named Hiel rebuilt the town of Jericho. But while Hiel was laying the foundation for the town wall, his oldest son Abiram died. And while he was finishing the gates, his youngest son Segub died. This happened just as the LORD had told Joshua to say many years ago." (1 Kings 16:34)

Eventually, the city of Jericho was successfully rebuilt and has survived throughout the region's tumultuous history. Today the city falls within Israel's borders and has a population of about 20,000.

above right: ***The Seven Trumpets of Jericho***
James Tissot (1836–1902)

PROPHETIC CURSES

Placing a curse on someone is just a silly superstition, according to some. For others, the mere thought of being cursed conjures an unexplained sense of dread or foreboding.

While shrouded in mystery, the practice of cursing someone is found throughout the Bible. Not long before Joshua announced a curse on anyone who rebuilt Jericho, his predecessor, Moses, promised a curse on the entire nation of Israel if they violated their covenant with God: *"Israel, today I am giving you the laws and teachings of the LORD your God. And if you don't obey them all, he will put many curses on you. Your businesses and farms will fail. You won't have enough bread to eat. You'll have only a few children, your crops will be small, and your herds of cattle and flocks of sheep and goats won't produce many young. The LORD will make you fail in everything you do"* (Deuteronomy 28:15–19).

Moses assured the people they need not fear, so long as they remained faithful to God. The blessings for obedience far outweighed the curses for disobedience (see Deuteronomy 7:6–15).

Jericho is believed to be one of the oldest cities in the world, dating back to 9000 BC. The Bible states that Jesus passed through Jericho, where he healed two blind men and converted a local tax collector named Zacchaeus. Christianity took hold in the city during the Byzantine era, and a church dedicated to Saint Eliseus was erected there.

Name Meaning	Moon
Founded	9000 BC
First Mentioned	Book of Numbers
Description	City of Palm Trees (Deuteronomy 34:3)

A Reading from Joshua 6:15–16, 20, 26–27

On the seventh day, the army got up at daybreak. They marched slowly around Jericho the same as they had done for the past six days, except on this day they went around seven times. Then the priests blew the trumpets, and Joshua yelled: "Get ready to shout! The LORD will let you capture this town. . . ."

The priests blew their trumpets again, and the soldiers shouted as loud as they could. The walls of Jericho fell flat. Then the soldiers rushed up the hill, went straight into the town, and captured it. . . .

After Jericho was destroyed, Joshua warned the people, "Someday a man will rebuild Jericho, but the LORD will put a curse on him, and the man's oldest son will die when he starts to build the town wall. And by the time he finishes the wall and puts gates in it, all his children will be dead." The LORD helped Joshua in everything he did, and Joshua was famous everywhere in Canaan.

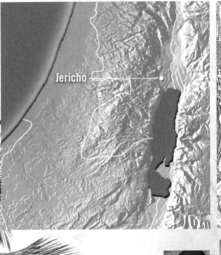

Jericho

RAHAB

The prostitute Rahab assisted the Israelite spies before the invasion of Jericho. She and her family were spared from death, and they were allowed to live among the Israelites. Rahab is listed in Matthew's genealogy as an ancestor of both Jesus and King David (Matthew 1:1–18).

POINT OF INTEREST

It is interesting to note that Jericho, located on the west side of the Jordan River, about ten miles north of the Dead Sea, is one of the oldest continuously inhabited cities in the world. It had existed and thrived a long time before Joshua's roundabout attack.

The Extraordinary Fall of Israel:
The Assyrian Conquest

Just two generations after the death of Israel's King David, the nation split in two. It was, in many ways, the beginning of the end.

Both the Northern and Southern kingdoms wandered away from the covenant forged in the desert between God and Moses following the Exodus. Courageous prophets spoke words of warning to kings and commoners alike, condemning the immorality of God's chosen people: their rampant idolatry, their exploitation of the poor, and other social ills.

There was no great mystery here; the prophets declared that by abandoning the covenant, the people of Israel would bring disaster on themselves. This judgment came in the form of conquerors from the east and the south—the Assyrians in the eighth century BC and the Babylonians in the sixth century BC.

The prophet Isaiah proclaimed these words from God: *"I am furious! And I will use the king of Assyria as a club to beat down you godless people"* (Isaiah 10:5–6). A few chapters later, in Isaiah 36, the prophet described the Assyrian's plan to attack Jerusalem, the capital of Judah (the Southern Kingdom).

The Bible recalls the fulfillment of this terrifying prophecy in the books of 2 Kings and 2 Chronicles. Both of these historical books detail generations of Israelite victories, defeats, misdeeds, and rulers.

Assyria attacked both the Northern and Southern kingdoms of Israel. The first attack came during the rule of Assyria's King Tiglath Pileser (2 Kings 15:19–20), the second during Assyrian King Shalmaneser's reign. It was the second attack that resulted in the destruction of Samaria, capital of the Northern Kingdom (2 Kings 17:5–6). The final Assyrian invasion of Judah is described in 2 Kings 18:13–37 and 2 Chronicles 32:1–19.

By the end of Assyrian King Sennacherib's rule, Isaiah's prophecy had come true. Assyria had wreaked havoc on both kingdoms of Israel.

READ IT FOR YOURSELF

2 KINGS 17:6b

The Assyrian king took the Israelites away to Assyria as prisoners. He forced some of them to live in the town of Halah, others to live near the Habor River in the territory of Gozan, and still others to live in towns where the Median people lived.

Assyrian fresco

Disaster Foretold:
The Fall of God's Holy City

HABAKKUK

One of the great mysteries concerning the fall of Israel is how God could use notoriously evil kingdoms like Assyria and Babylonia to execute judgment on his people. The Old Testament prophet Habakkuk wrestled with this very question, pleading with God not to allow these nations to *"gobble up people who are better than they are"* (Habakkuk 1:13).

God did not reveal to Habakkuk his reasons for using Assyria and Babylonia as instruments of judgment; however, he assured the troubled prophet that they, like Israel, would be made to answer for their evil deeds.

By the late 600s BC, Babylonia had grown into one of the world's dominant empires. Its king, Nebuchadnezzar, conquered Jerusalem in 586 BC—just as the prophets Isaiah and Jeremiah had warned.

More than a century before Jerusalem's fall, Isaiah warned Hezekiah, king of Judah, about the city's fate: *"I have a message for you from the LORD All-Powerful,"* Isaiah told the king. *"One day everything you and your ancestors have stored up will be taken to Babylonia. The LORD has promised that nothing will be left. Some of your own sons will be taken to Babylonia, where they will be disgraced and made to serve in the king's palace"* (Isaiah 39:5–7).

Jeremiah painted much the same picture, but with startlingly precise detail. He predicted the number of years the Israelites would spend in exile. *"This country will be as empty as a desert, because I will make all of you the slaves of the king of Babylonia for 70 years"* (Jeremiah 25:11).

According to the writer of 2 Kings, the Babylonian assault on Jerusalem began around 605 BC, with the final invasion toppling the city almost twenty years later (2 Kings 24:1,10; 25:1).

The writer of 2 Chronicles also recounted Jerusalem's fall to Babylonia: *"In the spring of the year, King Nebuchadnezzar of Babylonia had Jehoiachin arrested and taken to Babylon, along with more of the valuable items in the temple. Then Nebuchadnezzar appointed Zedekiah king of Judah"* (2 Chronicles 36:10). The events Isaiah and Jeremiah foretold, including the looting and destruction of the temple and the exile of King Hezekiah's descendants, had come to pass.

Destruction of Jerusalem under the Babylonian rule. Illustration from the Nuremberg Chronicle, 1493.

Exile and Restoration:
God's Secret Plan Revealed

In Israel's darkest hour, God revealed a plan to breathe new life into the surviving remnant of his people. Impossible as it seemed, God promised to give them a future of restoration, reconciliation, and rebuilding.

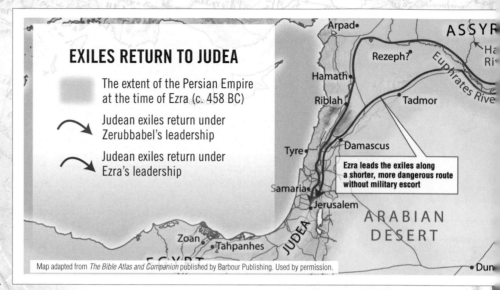

EXILES RETURN TO JUDEA

The extent of the Persian Empire at the time of Ezra (c. 458 BC)

Judean exiles return under Zerubbabel's leadership

Judean exiles return under Ezra's leadership

Ezra leads the exiles along a shorter, more dangerous route without military escort

Map adapted from *The Bible Atlas and Companion* published by Barbour Publishing. Used by permission.

This was Ezekiel's message from the Lord: *"But here is what I want you to tell the Israelites in Babylonia: It's true that I, the LORD God, have forced you out of your own country and made you live among foreign nations. But for now, I will be with you wherever you are, so that you can worship me. And someday, I will gather you from the nations where you are scattered and let you live in Israel again"* (Ezekiel 11:16–17).

The prophet Jeremiah also had a message of hope for the exiled people in Babylonia: *"After Babylonia has been the strongest nation for 70 years, I will be kind and bring you back to Jerusalem, just as I have promised. I will bless you with a future filled with hope—a future of success, not of suffering"* (Jeremiah 29:10–11).

Such a future must have been difficult to imagine from the vantage point of captivity. Still, according to the Old Testament scribe Ezra, King Cyrus of Persia overthrew the Babylonian Empire and issued a decree allowing the Israelites to return home and rebuild the temple in Jerusalem (Ezra 1:1–3).

Some biblical interpreters believe these mysterious words from the prophet Amos foretold the rebuilding of the temple: *"In the future, I will rebuild David's fallen kingdom. I will build it from its ruins and set it up again, just as it used to be"* (Amos 9:11). To the Israelites who returned to Jerusalem, the rebuilt temple symbolized their renewed relationship with God.

READ IT FOR YOURSELF

MICAH 4:6–8

The LORD said: "At that time I will gather my people—the lame and the outcasts, and all others to whose lives I have brought sorrow. Then the lame and the outcasts will belong to my people and become a strong nation. I, the LORD, will rule them from Mount Zion forever. Mount Zion in Jerusalem, guardian of my people, you will rule again."

top: The tower on the right side of the photograph is believed to be from the time of Nehemiah.

bottom: Cyrus restoring the vessels of the temple

left: **Nehemiah Looks Upon the Ruins of Jerusalem**, c. 1896–1902
James Tissot (1836–1902)

right: Israel despairing over the destruction of Jerusalem

READ IT FOR YOURSELF

ISAIAH 49:15–17

The LORD answered, "Could a mother forget a child who nurses at her breast? Could she fail to love an infant who came from her own body? Even if a mother could forget, I will never forget you. A picture of your city is drawn on my hand. You are always in my thoughts! Your city will be built faster than it was destroyed—those who attacked it will retreat and leave."

A miniature relief carving of King Cyrus of Persia

77

Babylonia:
The Great Fall

By the time that Babylonia had become a regional superpower and a growing threat to peace in the ancient Middle East, Israel had divided into the Northern and Southern kingdoms. Assyria, to the east, eventually conquered the Northern Kingdom (referred to as Israel). But it was Babylonia to the south (in what is southeastern Iraq today) that threatened the Southern Kingdom of Judah, eventually capturing Judah's capital, Jerusalem, and carrying its people into exile.

It was Babylon, the kingdom's capital, that served as the backdrop to the story of Daniel, a young exile who was among those taken from Jerusalem to be assimilated into the conquering culture, as was the custom of the day (Daniel 1). It was Babylonia that played a starring role in the ancient prophecies of men like Isaiah, Ezekiel, and Jeremiah.

Babylonia seemed unstoppable. That it would meet the same fate as Judah was inconceivable. Yet the prophet Isaiah, who lived in Judah at a time when Babylonia's military threat was escalating, predicted three things: that the Medes (from what is now northeastern Iran) would rise against Babylon, that Babylon would be destroyed just as surely as the cities of Sodom and Gomorrah had been centuries before, and that it would never be settled again, not even by wandering shepherds (Isaiah 13:17–22).

What happened next is mystifying indeed; but to historians, it is no secret.

Babylon was indeed captured by the Medes in 539 BC. It was completely ruined by the first century BC. Today, it is home to wild animals; it is mostly uninhabited except for traveling tourists or archaeologists. The city is described as a heap of rubble.

READ IT FOR YOURSELF

JEREMIAH 51:1–2, 36–37

I, the LORD, am sending a wind to destroy the people of Babylonia and Babylon, its capital. Foreign soldiers will come from every direction, and when the disaster is over, Babylonia will be empty and worthless. . . .

My people, I am on your side, and I will take revenge on Babylon. I will cut off its water supply, and its stream will dry up. Babylon will be a pile of rubble where only jackals live, and everyone will be afraid to walk among the ruins.

Detail of the Ishtar Gate

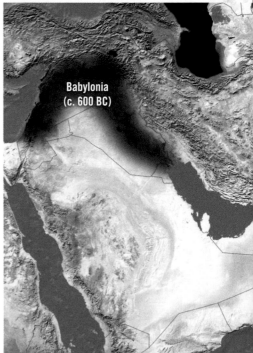
Babylonia (c. 600 BC)

Depiction of the fall of Babylon

The rise of Assyria brings into prominence the national god Ashur, who had been the city god of Asshur, the ancient capital.

All that remains today of the ancient famed city of Babylon is a mound, or tell, of broken mudbrick buildings and debris in the fertile Mesopotamian plain between the Tigris and Euphrates Rivers, in the country of Iraq.

Founder	Nimrod
Location	Euphrates

A Reading from Isaiah 47:5–7

Babylon, be silent! Sit in the dark. No longer will nations accept you as their queen. I was angry with my people. So I let you take their land and bring disgrace on them. You showed them no mercy, but were especially cruel to those who were old. You thought that you would be queen forever. You didn't care what you did; it never entered your mind that you might get caught.

POINT OF INTEREST

Considered one of the original Seven Wonders of the World, The Hanging Gardens were built by Nebuchadnezzar II around 600 BC near present-day Al Hillah in Iraq (formerly Babylon). He built the gardens to console his wife, who missed the natural surroundings of her homeland in Persia.

ADVISOR TO KINGS

Daniel first served in the court of the king Nebuchadnezzar along with his friends Hananiah (Shadrach), Mishael (Meshach), and Azariah (Abednego), and he quickly distinguished himself by his great learning and understanding. Later Daniel interpreted various dreams for Nebuchadnezzar and was rewarded with high promotions and wealth. Daniel also interpreted a divine message given to Nebuchadnezzar's son Belshazzar.

Daniel continued his distinguished government service even after the kingdom changed hands and was ruled by the Persians. Yet his devotion to God remained unshaken.

SAIAS · MOSES · DANIEL · DA VID · HI

CHAPTER 7

Unlikely Heroes:
The Improbable Rise of Bible Greats

The Bible is filled with astonishing tales of great deeds performed by larger-than-life characters. Many of these stories are so familiar that it's easy to gloss over their head-scratching mysteries—for example, Samson's impossible feats of strength, Solomon's mind-boggling wisdom, or Daniel's undisturbed night in the lions' den.

The secret to these heroes of the Bible—and their mighty acts—was that their faith, and their source of wisdom and strength, were evidence of their trust in the power of the one true God. They did not derive their power or courage from within themselves. Centuries later, their legacies, and their mystique, live on.

How did these unlikely heroes demonstrate the power of God at work by achieving the impossible?

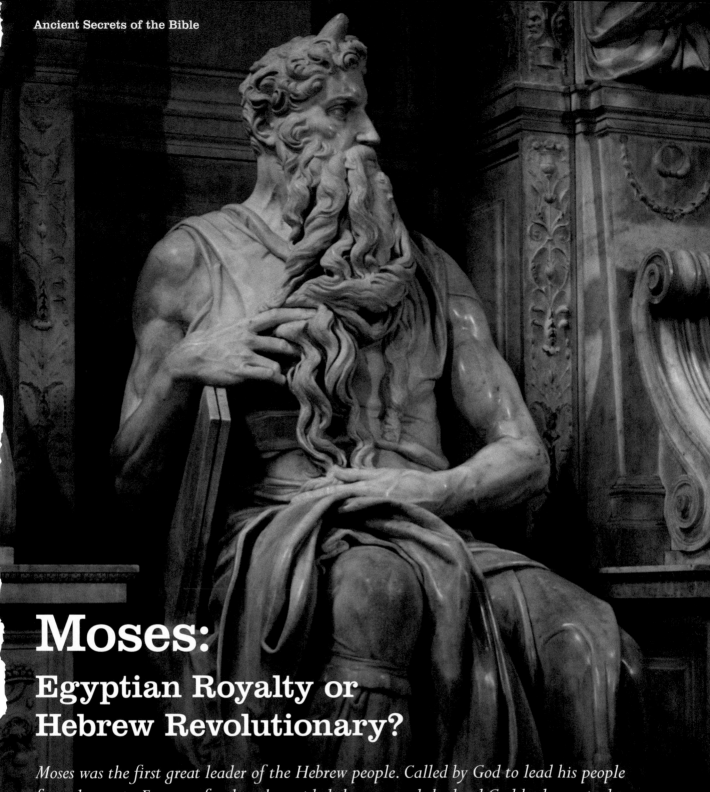

Moses:
Egyptian Royalty or Hebrew Revolutionary?

Moses was the first great leader of the Hebrew people. Called by God to lead his people from slavery in Egypt to freedom, he guided them toward the land God had promised to their ancestor Abraham. His commanding presence and proximity to God made him a towering figure for his people, yet they did not always heed his words. The first five books of the Bible are sometimes referred to as The Books of Moses, which Jews call the Law or the Torah; they are the sacred foundation of Judaism. Moses' life story is filled with strange miracles and marvels, but it also offers memorable depictions of the sad failings of human nature.

Moses was actually a Hebrew descendant of the people who immigrated to Egypt from Canaan. His ancestors, Jacob and his twelve sons, came to Egypt to survive a famine (Genesis 42–50). In the four centuries that followed their arrival, the family grew into a nation—but sadly, they became a nation enslaved to Egypt. At the time of Moses' birth, Pharaoh (the king of Egypt) had ordered the killing of male Hebrew babies as a brutal means of controlling the Israelites' increasing population; he feared they would one day ally themselves with Egypt's enemies and thereby escape. It was during this period that Moses was born, and Pharaoh's grim edict provided the backdrop for his first great escape.

BABY IN A BASKET

Moses escaped Pharaoh's order to kill Hebrew baby boys because his mother hid him in a basket at the edge of the Nile River. In a mystifying twist of providence, he was found and rescued—and his benefactor was an Egyptian princess who adopted him into the royal family (see Exodus 1–2). Thus Moses enjoyed the privileges of royalty and learned the protocols of Egypt's court, knowledge that served him well when he later faced Pharaoh as a petitioner for his people.

AN EXILE

From his infancy, Moses was thus intricately tied to two different worlds. He was raised as a child of royalty, yet was taken care of by a Hebrew nurse—who just happened to be his own mother! Since the Hebrews were oppressed by the Egyptian government, his loyalties were divided. When Moses witnessed an Egyptian beating a Hebrew, he cast his lot with the people of his birth: he killed the Egyptian—and he thought he had gotten away with it. The next day, though, he realized that his action had not gone unnoticed, putting the secret of his true identity at risk.

Pharaoh set out to kill Moses, but once again the wily young man escaped. Leaving behind everything he knew, Moses fled to the desert, where he became a shepherd, married, and had children. It seemed he had made a clean getaway and established a new life. Then he came upon a bush that seemed to be burning—though it never burned up—and heard the voice of God (see Exodus 2–3). Here was a call he could not escape. Moses had met his destiny.

A Reading from Exodus 8:20–25

The LORD said to Moses:

"Early tomorrow morning, while the king is on his way to the river, go and say to him, 'The LORD commands you to let his people go, so they can worship him. If you don't, he will send swarms of flies to attack you, your officials, and every citizen of your country. Your houses will be full of flies, and the ground will crawl with them.'

" 'The LORD's people in Goshen won't be bothered by flies, but your people in the rest of the country will be tormented by them. That's how you will know that the LORD is here in Egypt. This miracle will happen tomorrow.'"

The LORD kept his promise — the palace and the homes of the royal officials swarmed with flies, and the rest of the country was infested with them as well. Then the king sent for Moses and Aaron and told them, "Go ahead and sacrifice to your God, but stay here in Egypt."

ESCAPE ARTIST

Not once but three times Moses avoided near death at the hands of Pharaoh. His first two escapes—as a baby and later as an adult when he fled to the desert—were just shadows of Moses' greatest getaway, when he led the entire Hebrew nation through the Red Sea and out of Egypt. What was the secret to Moses' talent for evading Pharaoh? According to the book of Exodus, it was none other than the mighty hand of God.

Samson:

Secret Strength from a Strange Vow?

The ultimate Old Testament muscleman, Samson was one of twelve "judges," or military leaders, used by God to rescue the Israelites from their many oppressors. Samson's story began on a suitably mysterious note. His parents were visited by an angel who told them they were going to have a son who would rise up and defeat Israel's enemies, the Philistines. Was the secret of Samson's strength an enigmatic vow buried in the ancient Hebrew Scriptures?

NAZIRITE MYSTERY

In the book of Numbers (6:2–8), Moses gave instructions for anyone wishing to take a vow of dedication. To become a "Nazirite" was to become specially consecrated to God. Nazirites were not allowed to drink wine or other intoxicating drinks. They were not to cut their hair or touch a dead body.

Most Nazirite vows were temporary. In the New Testament, the apostle Paul is seen cutting his hair after the completion of one such vow. However, according to the angel who visited his parents, Samson was to be a Nazirite for life—permanently dedicated to God and to the liberation of his people.

SAMSON'S STRENGTH . . . AND WEAKNESS

How Samson's vow contributed to his great strength is a mystery. Certainly, such a vow of abstinence would strengthen a warrior's spirit, but that alone cannot explain Samson's superhuman powers. And what strength it was! He once tore a lion in half; another time he killed 1,000 Philistines using the jawbone of a donkey.

Desperate for revenge, the Philistines bargained with Samson's lover, Delilah, to uncover the source of Samson's secret strength. Delilah made a game of it, teasing Samson into giving her the reason for his strength.

Three times Samson gave her bogus answers—tie me up with seven bowstrings, use new ropes, weave my hair on a loom—but each time he used his strength to free himself.

Delilah continued to pester Samson until he finally revealed his secret: *"I have belonged to God ever since I was born, so my hair has never been cut. If it were ever cut off, my strength would leave me, and I would be as weak as anyone else"* (Judges 16:17).

Delilah shared Samson's secret with his enemies, and while he was sleeping, she proceeded to cut off his seven braids. When Samson awoke, his strength was gone. The Philistines overpowered him easily: *"The Philistines grabbed Samson and poked out his eyes. They took him to the prison in Gaza and chained him up. Then they put him to work, turning a millstone to grind grain"* (Judges 16:21).

But the Philistines didn't cut his hair again, and it started growing back—and so did his strength. Samson had gambled away his leadership and his influence, but even in death, he brought scores of Philistines to justice. Whatever his human faults, he stands out as one of the Bible's superheroes.

THE TRUE SECRET OF SAMSON'S STRENGTH

Samson believed his long hair was the source of his strength, but his biographer suggested the real secret lay elsewhere and provided this clue when describing the moment that Samson was overpowered by the Philistines: *"Samson woke up and thought, 'I'll break loose and escape, just as I always do.' He did not realize that the LORD had stopped helping him"* (Judges 16:20). According to the writer of Judges, Samson's superhuman strength came from God—not his hair.

A Reading from Judges 16:15–17

"Samson," Delilah said, "you claim to love me, but you don't mean it! You've made me look like a fool three times now, and you still haven't told me why you are so strong."

Delilah started nagging and pestering him day after day, until he couldn't stand it any longer.

Finally, Samson told her the truth. "I have belonged to God ever since I was born, so my hair has never been cut. If it were ever cut off, my strength would leave me, and I would be as weak as anyone else."

Solomon:

The Legendary Wisdom of Israel's Most Renowned King

What made Solomon, King David's son, so wise? The book of 1 Kings holds the answer to this puzzle. At the outset of Solomon's reign, God invited him to ask for any gift he desired. Little did Solomon know, it was a test—and he passed with flying colors by requesting not wealth but wisdom. Because God was pleased with his request, he granted Solomon not only wisdom but also riches, power, respect, and influence.

One of Solomon's most famous judgments involved returning a baby to his mother. Two women laid claim to the same child. When Solomon ordered that the baby be cut in half, and that each woman be given half the child, the real mother cried out. The other (who was accused of accidentally killing her own son, then switching the babies) was willing to let the child die. Solomon's ploy revealed the truth.

A VISITOR FROM THE EAST

The queen of Sheba, ruler of a land in southwestern Arabia that maintained a trade alliance with Israel, traveled to Solomon's palace to see for herself if his reputation as the wisest man in the world was deserved. According to the Bible, she went to Jerusalem, the capital city, to test Solomon with the most difficult questions. Solomon was able to meet every challenge and answer every riddle:

"The Queen was amazed at Solomon's wisdom. She was breathless when she saw his palace, the food on his table, his officials, all his servants in their uniforms, and the sacrifices he offered at the LORD's *temple.*

"She said: 'Solomon, in my own country I had heard about your wisdom and all you've done. But I didn't believe it until I saw it with my own eyes! And there's so much I didn't hear about. You are greater than I was told'" (2 Chronicles 9:3–6).

SOLOMON'S WISDOM: VANISHED WITHOUT A TRACE

Solomon appears to have been wiser in his youth than as a grown man. What became of his legendary wisdom? It apparently led to great financial and diplomatic success; and as they so often do in this world, Solomon's growing wealth and power revealed fault lines in his character, and his follies began to match his riches. Therein lies the answer to the mystery of Solomon's vanishing wisdom.

At the height of his kingdom, Solomon had 700 wives and 300 concubines, many from other countries. In that day, polygamy built relations between countries, but it was not the rule among the Hebrews. Besotted with his enormous harem, Solomon let his many wives lull him into foreign forms of worship. According to his own story, Solomon's wisdom had come from his faithful union with God. By the end of his reign, though, he loved his wives and riches more than he loved God.

The book of Proverbs, part of which Solomon wrote, extols the positive values of a God-centered life, but later writings, for example Ecclesiastes, which some attributed to Solomon, lament the futility of life lived in pursuit of everything except God. In his disillusionment, Solomon seemed to come full circle: *"Respect and obey God! This is what life is all about"* (Ecclesiastes 12:13).

If the real test of a nation's leader is the legacy he or she leaves behind, Solomon failed. Exhausted from the amount of work it took to support Solomon's extravagant ways, his people lost their faith in their leader. After Solomon died, his kingdom was split in two: for all his early wisdom and later riches, he left behind an Israel whose house was divided.

A Reading from 1 Kings 4:30–34

[Solomon] was wiser than anyone else in the world, including the wisest people of the east and of Egypt…. Solomon became famous in every country around Judah and Israel. Solomon wrote 3,000 wise sayings and composed more than 1,000 songs. He could talk about all kinds of plants, from large trees to small bushes, and he taught about animals, birds, reptiles, and fish. Kings all over the world heard about Solomon's wisdom and sent people to listen to him teach.

Scene of King Solomon from the *Bible of Charles the Bald,* c. 880 Ingobertus

Esther:
The Beauty Queen with a Dangerous Secret

Most heroes of the Old Testament were men——no surprise, given the privileged status men enjoyed in the ancient Near East. But there are a few notable exceptions: Deborah, one of twelve judges who rescued Israel from oppression; Ruth, who became great-grandmother to Israel's greatest ruler, David; and the widow-turned-warrior Judith, whose story is featured in most Roman Catholic and Orthodox Bibles. Perhaps most famous of all is Esther, a Jewish girl who became queen of Persia, hiding a secret identity that could have gotten her killed.

Esther was a young Jewish girl caught up in a double life. To the casual reader, God seems mysteriously absent from her story; Esther is the only book in the Bible that does not mention God by name. However, most Jewish and Christian readers see God at work behind the scenes, using Esther to save the Jewish people from extermination.

FROM ORPHAN TO QUEEN TO SAVIOR

Esther, who was originally named Hadassah, was orphaned at an early age and adopted by her cousin Mordecai, a Jew who occupied a high position in the court of Xerxes, the king of Persia (modern-day Iran and Iraq), at a time when there were many Jews living in that nation. Hadassah was beautiful, lively, and intelligent; she caught the eye of the king, who did not know she was a Jew. Mordecai urged Hadassah to keep her true identity a secret, and she complied by only using her Persian name, Esther. Some time after the marriage, Mordecai learned that two of the king's advisers were planning to murder him; he told Esther, who alerted Xerxes, saving his life—and earning further royal favor for both Mordecai and Esther.

Esther and Ahasuerus (Xerxes)
Francesco Fontebasso (1709–1769)
Parish Church, Povo, Italy

Xerxes's chief minister, Haman, grew jealous of Mordecai's increasing influence, and he concocted a plan to massacre Mordecai and all the Jews then living in Persia, in a single day. But after Esther and Mordecai learned of the scheme, Esther outwitted Haman and convinced Xerxes of Haman's wickedness. In the end, Haman was hanged on the very gallows he had ordered built for the execution of Mordecai. All the Jews of Persia were saved, and some 75,000 of Haman's troops and followers across the land were put to death. The Jews then celebrated their deliverance with a triumphant celebration called Purim—a Babylonian term for the lots that Haman used to determine the day on which the attack against the Jews was to take place.

ESTHER'S FEAST: PURIM

Thousands of years after Esther's story was first told, the feast of Purim remains one of the most joyous annual events on the Jewish calendar. Readings from the book of Esther are a highlight of Purim, with the villain Haman often being loudly booed by the congregation in the synagogue, while the heroic Esther and Mordecai are cheered. The feast often features an exchange of gifts; the playing of harmless pranks; and parades with masked characters dressed as Haman, Esther, and others from the story. With its tale of survival in an alien land, the book of Esther reminds Jews of their long history of wandering and of the times when they were delivered from evil by God's hand, as in the story of Moses and the first Passover. The largest modern American Jewish women's service organization, Hadassah, takes its name from Esther's original Hebrew name.

A Reading from Esther 9:25–27

Esther went to King Xerxes and asked him to save her people. Then the king gave written orders for Haman and his sons to be punished in the same terrible way that Haman had in mind for the Jews. So they were hanged. Mordecai's letter had said that the Jews must celebrate for two days because of what had happened to them. This time of celebration is called Purim, which is the Hebrew word for the lots that were cast. Now every year the Jews set aside these two days for having parties and celebrating, just as they were told to do.

Daniel:
Quiet Defiance, Impossible Survival

Most superheroes of the Bible are distinguished by their mighty deeds, but Daniel was a quieter sort of hero. After being carried into captivity by the Babylonians, Daniel and his friends faced immense pressure to assimilate——to embrace Babylonian values and religion. They refused. Instead, they became powerful rulers in Babylon while still remaining true to their faith.

As was the custom of the day, when the Babylonians conquered Judah, the best and brightest Jews were taken back and assimilated into Babylon. This policy advanced Babylon's strength, and also assured that Judah's best warriors weren't left behind in the homeland to lead a revolt.

Daniel came as a captive, but he assimilated to Persian life and culture. He even acquired political power and respect—but without giving up the foundational precepts of his faith. He continued to follow the dietary restrictions that God had placed on his people, the Jews, and he continued to worship in the way he was taught as a child. This faithfulness was not just a sacrifice for him and his friends; it landed him in hot water—and his friends in a hot furnace. Daniel was thrown into a lions' den for praying to God. His friends were thrown into a fiery furnace for refusing to worship idols. The great mystery is, how did they survive?

DANIEL'S FRIENDS AND THE FIERY FURNACE

Daniel's friends were thrown into a furnace that was probably used for smelting ore. They had disobeyed King Nebuchadnezzar's decree and had to take the heat! So did they survive through some sleight of hand, or were there unseen forces at work?

Was the escape from the fiery furnace any more spectacular than a firewalker's stunt? Ordinary people have shown they can scurry across hot coals without getting burned. Actually, though, firewalkers move quickly over ash-coated coals that have cooled down below 500°F. Daniel's friends strolled leisurely in a furnace blazing at nearly 2000°F—hot enough to kill the soldiers who threw them into it. Yet they survived. (Read Daniel 3.)

DANIEL'S ESCAPE FROM THE HUNGRY LIONS

When lions aren't hungry, they are content to lie basking in the sun for up to twenty hours a day. A man might survive in a den of lions whose stomachs were full. But in a den of hungry lions, odds are he wouldn't last an hour. What chance would he have against beasts that stand nearly fifty inches high, weigh more than 400 pounds, have razor-like claws, and two-inch teeth? These sinewy predators can take down a 900-pound zebra!

So when Daniel was placed in a lions' den as his punishment for not praying to the king's gods, how did he survive? He couldn't leave the pit, because it was sealed with a stone. He had nothing with which to keep the lions at bay—no whip, no chair. Could the lions have just been fed? Evidently not—for after Daniel was released from the den, the men who had accused him of wrongdoing were thrown into it, and the lions attacked them all immediately. (Read Daniel 6.)

A Reading from Daniel 6:19–23

At daybreak the king got up and ran to the pit. He was anxious and shouted, "Daniel, you were faithful and served your God. Was he able to save you from the lions?"

Daniel answered, "Your Majesty, I hope you live forever! My God knew that I was innocent, and he sent an angel to keep the lions from eating me. Your Majesty, I have never done anything to hurt you."

The king was relieved to hear Daniel's voice, and he gave orders for him to be taken out of the pit. Daniel's faith in his God had kept him from being harmed.

Blast furnace

Daniel in the lions' den

Daniel's story also appears in two Apocryphal books: *Susanna* and *Bel and the Dragon*.

CHAPTER 8

The End of the World: Unlocking the Future

Images of angels descending, great trumpets sounding, terrifying judgments being unleashed, people standing before a great white throne of judgment—the Bible's depiction of the end boggles the mind. Undoubtedly, these images seem strange and mysterious to most readers; but whatever we make of them, at least one thing can be discerned: someday, God will make the final judgment on right and wrong.

To the first-century men and women who encountered the writings and proclamation of the Early Church, Jesus' promise to return, called the Second Coming, carried with it the hope that justice would be done and faith rewarded.

However, the precise events surrounding the end are shrouded in secrecy. Perhaps no other biblical subject generates as much curiosity and debate as the "end times."

When—and how—will the end come about?

The Empty Throne (Second Coming of Christ)
6th century AD. Early Christian.

Watching and Waiting:

Looking for the Great Hope

READ IT FOR YOURSELF

JOHN 14:1–3

Jesus said to his disciples, "Don't be worried! Have faith in God and have faith in me. There are many rooms in my Father's house. I wouldn't tell you this, unless it was true. I am going there to prepare a place for each of you. After I have done this, I will come back and take you with me. Then we will be together."

Last Judgment
Michelangelo Buonarroti (1475–1564)

The pages of the New Testament ring with hope—the unshakable conviction that Jesus will return for his followers. Even so, the exact timing of his return is a secret that even the biblical writers could not unlock.

The expectation of a triumphant return can be traced to Jesus himself. Matthew's Gospel records a conversation between Jesus and his disciples on the Mount of Olives, during which Jesus revealed what the disciples could expect in the future. The events described by Jesus would culminate in his return: *"And there will be the Son of Man. All nations on earth will weep when they see the Son of Man coming on the clouds of heaven with power and great glory"* (Matthew 24:30; see also Mark 13:24–27; Luke 21:25–28).

Yet in practically the same breath, Jesus warned that no one—not even the Son of Man—would be able to unlock the secret of his coming: *"No one knows the day or hour. The angels in heaven don't know, and the Son himself doesn't know. Only the Father knows"* (Matthew 24:36). For nearly two millennia, many have tried to predict the timing of Jesus' return; all have failed.

A few decades after Jesus returned to his Father in heaven, the apostle Paul wrote a letter to Christians in Thessalonica. It's clear from his letter that Paul did not view the return of Jesus as some faraway event; it was something on which he hinged his present hope. Paul expected that Christ would return during his readers' lifetime (1 Thessalonians 4:13–18). But in his next letter to the same church, Paul adjusted this apocalyptic forecast by saying that a series of startling events would take place before Christ's return (2 Thessalonians 2:1–12).

Similar to a warning Jesus gave his disciples (Matthew 24:42–44), Paul compared the return of Christ to a nighttime thief arriving unexpectedly (1 Thessalonians 5:1–2)—the implication being that Jesus' followers should live in a state of constant readiness, knowing that day may come at any time (1 Thessalonians 5:4–8).

Even though the timing of Christ's return is wrapped in secrecy, Jesus made clear that no one would be able to miss the event itself. Prophesying from the Mount of Olives, Jesus promised that his return would be spectacular and visible to all (Matthew 24:27).

Today, Christians continue to speculate on the details surrounding Jesus' return. Some believe it will set into motion other events, such as the taking up of Christians to heaven (sometimes called "the rapture"), the overpowering of evil (Revelation 20:1–3), and an extended period in which Jesus will rule on earth (Revelation 20:4–6). The debate over Christ's return will most likely continue until the event itself. Despite all the mystery, however, Christians continue to look forward to the great hope of a future world where Christ will reign over all (Matthew 19:28–30).

Ascension
Folio 13v of the *Rabbula Gospels*
(Florence, Biblioteca Mediceo Laurenziana, cod. Plut. I, 560)

A Reading from
1 Thessalonians 4:13–18

My friends, we want you to understand how it will be for those followers who have already died. Then you won't grieve over them and be like people who don't have any hope. We believe Jesus died and was raised to life. We also believe that when God brings Jesus back again, he will bring with him all who had faith in Jesus before they died. Our Lord Jesus told us that when he comes, we won't go up to meet him ahead of his followers who have already died.

With a loud command and with the shout of the chief angel and a blast of God's trumpet, the Lord will return from heaven. Then those who had faith in Christ before they died will be raised to life. Next, all of us who are still alive will be taken up into the clouds together with them to meet the Lord in the sky. From that time on we will all be with the Lord forever. Encourage each other with these words.

Until That Day:
Suffering and Survival

The book of Acts documents the rapid growth of the Early Church. With this growth came recognition—a visibility that sometimes resulted in persecution. But the Christian Church has endured. Both the suffering and the survival of the Church were prophesied in Scripture.

During his time on earth, Jesus talked about the persecution his followers could expect. They would be hated, Jesus warned (John 15:18). He also promised that those who remained faithful would survive (Matthew 10:22). Jesus was persecuted and killed because of his teachings, and he told his followers to prepare for the same treatment. Amazingly, however, he also told them not to despair; persecution for doing what is right is a part of what it means to be faithful—and will be rewarded by God (Matthew 5:10–12).

Jesus spoke these prophecies prior to his own suffering and death. They proved true almost immediately after the Church was born. As a result of persecution, Jesus' first followers in Jerusalem scattered throughout the region (Acts 5:17–42; 8:1). Paradoxically, the book of Acts reports that the Church grew in proportion to its suffering (for example, see Acts 6:1, 7; 16:5).

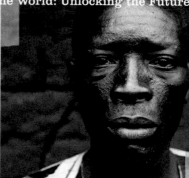

In 1 Peter, a letter traditionally ascribed by many to the apostle Peter, who was martyred for following Jesus, believers are told that their suffering is no great mystery: *"Don't be surprised or shocked that you are going through testing that is like walking through fire"* (1 Peter 4:12). The argument presented is that suffering somehow connects Christians more intimately to Christ.

Still, Jesus' followers take heart when they remember his promise that not even death can overpower the Church (Matthew 16:18). In the book of Revelation, John of Patmos describes both the Church's endurance until the very end of days and the rewards for those who withstand persecution (Revelation 3:8–11; 7:9–17).

Persecution is not the only threat to the Church, according to the New Testament. Jesus warned his followers that false messiahs and prophets would try to fool God's people by working miracles and signs (Matthew 24:4–5, 23–24; see also Mark 13:5–6, 21–22).

They would claim to teach God's truth, but would in fact lead people away from the truth. The Bible has a word for people like this: antichrist—literally, "false messiah."

Jesus' warning is not the Bible's first reference to an antichrist. The Old Testament book of Daniel mentions a ruler who would come and persecute the people of God (Daniel 7:25). Some claim this prophecy was fulfilled when the Greek ruler Antiochus IV Epiphanes came to power (175–164 BC) and brutally oppressed the Jewish people. Others insist that its ultimate fulfillment is still to come—in the person referred to later as the antichrist.

The secret of the antichrist only deepens in the New Testament. In his second letter to the church at Thessalonica, Paul describes in detail someone called *"the wicked one,"* which may be a reference to the antichrist. This person will bring destruction; he will be boastful; he will oppose everything that is holy. He will sit in God's temple, claim to be God, and fool people into following him instead of Jesus (2 Thessalonians 2:1–12). But Paul predicts this person will be no match for Jesus, who *"will kill him simply by breathing on him"* (2 Thessalonians 2:8).

Revelation 13:1–10 describes a beast from the sea with characteristics similar to those of *"the wicked one"* mentioned in 2 Thessalonians. This leads many to identify the beast described in Revelation as the antichrist. If this is the case, the prophecy about the antichrist may be one that is yet to be completely fulfilled.

Others believe the antichrist is not a single person; rather, anyone who teaches what the New Testament writers regarded as a false gospel is an antichrist. In two New Testament letters we read that false prophets had begun to appear late in the first century. These letters offer two rather straightforward markers for identifying such false prophets:

- They deny that Jesus is the Son of God (1 John 2:18–27).
- They deny Jesus' true humanity (1 John 4:1–3; 2 John 7).

READ IT FOR YOURSELF

ACTS 5:27–33, 40–41

When the apostles were brought before the council, the high priest said to them, "We told you plainly not to teach in the name of Jesus. But look what you have done! You have been teaching all over Jerusalem, and you are trying to blame us for his death."

Peter and the apostles replied:

"We don't obey people. We obey God. You killed Jesus by nailing him to a cross. But the God our ancestors worshiped raised him to life and made him our Leader and Savior. Then God gave him a place at his right side, so that the people of Israel would turn back to him and be forgiven. We are here to tell you about all this, and so is the Holy Spirit, who is God's gift to everyone who obeys God."

When the council members heard this, they became so angry they wanted to kill the apostles.

…

They called the apostles back in. They had them beaten with a whip and warned them not to speak in the name of Jesus. Then they let them go. The apostles left the council and were happy, because God had considered them worthy to suffer for the sake of Jesus.

A Great Tribulation

Surviving a night in a lions' den was enough to make the Old Testament prophet Daniel famous, but he was also highly regarded as an interpreter of dreams, a channel for prophetic messages from God. Many of these cryptic prophecies may refer to future events related to the final days before God completes his work in the world.

READ IT FOR YOURSELF

REVELATION 7:13–17

One of the elders asked me, "Do you know who these people are that are dressed in white robes? Do you know where they come from?"

"Sir," I answered, "you must know."

Then he told me:

"These are the ones who have gone through the great suffering. They have washed their robes in the blood of the Lamb and have made them white.

"And so they stand before the throne of God and worship him in his temple day and night. The one who sits on the throne will spread his tent over them.

"They will never hunger or thirst again, and they won't be troubled by the sun or any scorching heat.

"The Lamb in the center of the throne will be their shepherd. He will lead them to streams of life-giving water, and God will wipe all tears from their eyes."

While Daniel envisioned a glorious end, complete with God's absolute victory over evil and the restoration of a perfect world, this happy ending will not come easily, he counseled (Daniel 12; see also Matthew 25; Revelation 20–22).

The seer and prophet Daniel warned of suffering and destruction that must take place before God's work is complete (Daniel 9:20–27). These apocalyptic sayings are often referred to as the "Seventy Weeks" because they hint at seventy weeks of suffering to be experienced by the Israelites. According to the messenger in Daniel's dreams, the suffering is a punishment that will usher in the disappearance of evil and the rule of justice (Daniel 9:24). Biblical scholars interpret the description of the Seventy Weeks in different ways. It is unclear whether the weeks are literal or figurative—much less how many of them have already taken place. But Daniel indicates the suffering will increase until the archangel Michael comes to protect God's children from the world around them (Daniel 12:1).

In words reminiscent of Daniel, Jesus warned his followers that they would experience an unparalleled time of suffering (Mark 13:19). Some interpreters think this refers to Daniel's prophecy of the final "week" (Daniel 9:27) and the tribulation described in Revelation—a time of suffering for Christians prior to Jesus' return (Revelation 7:13–17; see also Matthew 24:15–22). Others believe that Christians will be spared this. John's apocalyptic vision in Revelation describes this period of suffering in vivid but puzzling detail (Revelation 6–19).

JUSTICE & JUDGMENT

The Bible represents God as just. Justice demands accountability—that is, judgment. The Old Testament prophets anticipated a final day of judgment. They called it by different names—*"that terrible day"* (Zephaniah 1:14), *"the day . . . will be like a red-hot furnace—with flames that burn up proud and sinful people, as though they were straw"* (Malachi 4:1), or *"the day when . . . all will be darkness"* (Amos 5:18). Their prophecies describe judgment as a day of reckoning for all the nations of the world, as well as for individuals who will be held accountable for the way they lived their lives (Isaiah 3:10–11).

Vision of St. John the Evangelist on Patmos
Jacobello Alberegno (d.1397)

In the New Testament, the teachings of the prophets merge seamlessly with Jesus' teachings. The Son of Man, Jesus told his disciples, would come to sit on his throne and separate the nations like sheep and goats—sheep on his right and goats on his left. The sheep would be those who are blessed because of the way they lived. The goats would be those who receive judgment (Matthew 25:31–46).

Compounding the mystery further is the apocalyptic drama in Revelation; it provides more details, but raises almost as many questions as it answers. John described how Jesus will judge the wicked and the righteous after his return. It is at this final judgment that Jesus will destroy death and evil forever—and that the salvation of the righteous will be complete (Revelation 20). The precise details of when and how this will happen are known only to God.

While the Bible presents the judgment of God as inevitable, it also offers certain hope of rescue from that judgment. First Peter, a letter traditionally ascribed to Jesus' disciple Peter, states, *"Put all your hope in how God will treat you with undeserved grace when Jesus Christ appears"* (1 Peter 1:13).

As the apocalyptic drama unfolds in Revelation, the great judgment day is followed by the creation of a new heaven and a new earth, where God's people live with him forever (Revelation 21:1–7).

READ IT FOR YOURSELF

REVELATION 21:1–7

I saw a new heaven and a new earth. The first heaven and the first earth had disappeared, and so had the sea. Then I saw New Jerusalem, the holy city, coming down from God in heaven. It was like a bride dressed in her wedding gown and ready to meet her husband.

I heard a loud voice shout from the throne:

"God's home is now with his people. He will live with them, and they will be his own. Yes, God will make his home among his people. He will wipe all tears from their eyes, and there will be no more death, suffering, crying, or pain. These things of the past are gone forever."

Then the one sitting on the throne said:

"I am making everything new. Write down what I have said. My words are true and can be trusted. Everything is finished! I am Alpha and Omega, the beginning and the end. I will freely give water from the life-giving fountain to everyone who is thirsty. All who win the victory will be given these blessings. I will be their God, and they will be my people."

far left:
Angel of the Revelation, c.1803–1805
William Blake

immediate left:
Vision of St. John the Evangelist on Patmos
Jacob Jordaens (1593–1678)

But Will It Come to Pass?

Fulfillment of the Promise

Reading about fulfilled prophecy can be exhilarating. But what about those yet to be fulfilled? Is biblical prophecy a relic of a bygone era? Is it the stuff of myth and legend, or will the end truly come about as described in Scripture?

ONE FOOT IN TWO WORLDS

If nothing else, the prophecies of the Bible offer hope, the idea that we can expect something else from our lives, something better. The apostle Paul, writer of many New Testament letters, told his readers that they were no longer citizens of this world only, but *"citizens of heaven"* as well (Ephesians 2:19–22; Philippians 3:20–21). It is only natural that a citizen of heaven would long for a bit of paradise.

Yet faith is not meant to be a form of fanatic escapism. The paradox of Christianity is that it involves looking ahead to the future while living meaningfully in the present (for example, see 2 Thessalonians 3:12). Taken as a whole, the Bible describes God's people as those who live fully in the here and now—the abundant life offered by Jesus—and at the same time hope for the future promises still to come.

In some ways, Christ's followers today find themselves in a similar position to the members of the Early Church. They have received the same promises as the ones we read in the New Testament—promises that Jesus would come again and justice would prevail once and for all. As far as those first believers knew, the fulfillment of these promises was just around the corner. They had no idea that nearly two thousand years would pass—and that we would still be waiting for it to come about.

The hidden meaning of biblical prophecy is discussed and debated today, much as it might have been in the early days of the Church. But whether one regards these prophetic texts as symbolic or literal, it's important to recall that there seemed to be a greater issue weighing on the minds of the prophets themselves—that is, how people choose to live their lives as they wait for the prophecies to be fulfilled.

The true purpose of biblical prophecy is not hidden or shrouded in mystery. If a new world is coming and everyone will be held accountable for the way they lived, the ultimate question the prophets would have us ask is this: In what manner are we living? Are we looking ahead eagerly? Are we prepared for whatever the future holds? Are we living a life of patient service and joyful proclamation as we wait?

Biblical prophecy, by its very nature, assumes there is a place outside of time and a divine being not bound by the unfolding of human history. The past, present, and future are connected. The great mystery is not that prophecy predicts the future; it is that it somehow connects our world—the days, weeks, months, years, and the events that fill them—with a place and a God who is bigger than time.

READ IT FOR YOURSELF

2 PETER 3:10–14

The day of the Lord's return will surprise us like a thief. The heavens will disappear with a loud noise, and the heat will melt the whole universe. Then the earth and everything on it will be seen for what they are.

Everything will be destroyed. So you should serve and honor God by the way you live. You should look forward to the day when God judges everyone, and you should try to make it come soon. On that day the heavens will be destroyed by fire, and everything else will melt in the heat. But God has promised us a new heaven and a new earth, where justice will rule. We are really looking forward to this!

My friends, while you are waiting, you should make certain that the Lord finds you pure, spotless, and living at peace.

JOHN 10:10

"A thief comes only to rob, kill, and destroy. I came so that everyone would have life, and have it fully."

CHAPTER 9

Guardian of Secrets:

The Origins of the Bible

The Bible, a repository of sacred mysteries, is itself a mystery. That it even exists—that its ancient texts have survived down the centuries—defies comprehension. Unlike sacred writings such as the Koran and the Book of Mormon, the Bible had no single person as its author. In fact, over an estimated 1,600 years, 40 different authors from all walks of life—including kings, shepherds, priests, prophets, a physician, and several fishermen—composed the books found in the Old and New Testaments. They wrote in Hebrew, Aramaic, and Greek.

To those for whom the Bible is a holy book, the secret to its enduring power lies in its divine inspiration. The Bible has survived all these years, many believe, because God has breathed life into its poetry, history, laws, and teachings.

Where did the Bible come from?
Who decided its contents?
And why is its power still felt today?

Revealed Over Time

The Bible came together over centuries. Some of its texts contained hidden meanings that came to be understood with the passage of time.

The earliest books of the Bible may have been passed on by word of mouth, with little change, from as early as 1400 BC—approximately 3,500 years ago! Some parts of the Old Testament may have reached their final written form as late as the end of the second century before the birth of Jesus.

The New Testament was composed over a much shorter period. Many scholars accept that all its books, from Matthew to Revelation, were written in less than one hundred years—and less than a century after Jesus' execution.

The meaning of these ancient texts was not always immediately clear. Sometimes, their interpretation evolved with time. For example, the Old Testament prophets often spoke of a Messiah, a divinely anointed deliverer who would come to save God's people. When the Gospel writers penned their accounts, they applied several Old Testament prophecies directly to Jesus: for example, his birth in Bethlehem (Micah 5:2; Matthew 2:1), his silence in the face of death (Isaiah 53:7; Matthew 27:11–14), the fate of his clothes at the hands of his oppressors (Psalm 22:18; John 19:23–24).

A Reading from 2 Timothy 3:16

Everything in the Scriptures is God's Word. All of it is useful for teaching and helping people and for correcting them and showing them how to live.

The word *Bible* is derived from the Greek word *biblia*, meaning "books."

Portions of the Bible have been translated into more than 2,500 languages and dialects—more than any other book in history—and the complete Bible is available in over 400 languages.

STORY OF THE TESTAMENTS

The Holy Bible consists of two major sections, the Old and New Testaments. Three major world religions trace their roots to the ancient Hebrew Scriptures known to Christians as the Old Testament.

To Muslims the Old Testament is a revered and historical source. To Jews it is the God-given Tanakh, or Hebrew Bible, comprised of three main sections: the Law, the Prophets, and the Writings. To Christians, the Old Testament is the sacred beginning of God's revelation, the history of a chosen people who look forward to the promised Messiah.

The first five books of the Bible, or the Torah, trace their beginnings to the story of one of Israel's early leaders, Moses. Over the next ten centuries, prophets, kings, court historians, shepherds, priests, and other faithful Jews captured the dramatic story of a chosen people, the Israelites, and their revelations and teachings about their one true God.

Between the Old and New Testaments, there was a mysterious, 400-year gap—or so it seemed. In fact, it was during this time that a number of additional books (those recognized by the Catholic and Orthodox churches and referred to as the Deuterocanon or Apocrypha by many Protestants) were written.

The New Testament was written in a comparatively short period of time after Jesus Christ's life on earth—from AD 50 to around AD 100. It is Christianity's account of the birth, life, death, and resurrection of Jesus and the creation of the Church he founded. The New Testament also contains teachings on how to live as a Christian, one who follows Christ.

Somehow, though stretched over centuries and expressed through many different writers, there is one universal message conveyed in the Bible from its first book, Genesis, to its last, Revelation: the Creator loves his creatures and has provided a way for them to know him and be one with him. The Bible is a road map for that spiritual journey.

HEBREW BIBLE (OLD TESTAMENT IN CHRISTIAN BIBLES)
Genesis
Exodus
Leviticus
Numbers
Deuteronomy
Joshua
Judges
Ruth
1 Samuel
2 Samuel
1 Kings
2 Kings
1 Chronicles
2 Chronicles
Ezra
Nehemiah
Esther
Job
Psalms
Proverbs
Ecclesiastes
Song of Songs
Isaiah
Jeremiah
Lamentations
Ezekiel
Daniel
Hosea
Joel
Amos
Obadiah
Jonah
Micah
Nahum
Habakkuk
Zephaniah
Haggai
Zechariah
Malachi

DEUTEROCANONICAL/ APOCRYPHAL BOOKS*
Tobit
Judith
Esther (Greek version)
Wisdom of Solomon
Sirach (Ecclesiasticus)
Baruch
Letter of Jeremiah
Prayer of Azariah and Song of the Three Jews
Susanna
Bel and the Dragon
1 Maccabees
2 Maccabees
1 Esdras
Prayer of Manasseh
Psalm 151
3 Maccabees
2 Esdras
4 Maccabees

*These books are excluded from the Hebrew Bible. Some of them, the deuterocanonical books, are included in Catholic and Orthodox Old Testament canons.

NEW TESTAMENT BOOKS
Matthew
Mark
Luke
John
Acts
Romans
1 Corinthians
2 Corinthians
Galatians
Ephesians
Philippians
Colossians
1 Thessalonians
2 Thessalonians
1 Timothy
2 Timothy
Titus
Philemon
Hebrews
James
1 Peter
2 Peter
1 John
2 John
3 John
Jude
Revelation

Safeguarding the Text

The Judean Wilderness

How did an ancient collection of books remain so remarkably well-preserved through the ages? It was the work of anonymous scribes—diligent sentinels whose unceasing toil ensured the survival of these sacred texts.

Both Jewish and Christian scribes approached their exacting task as a sacred mission, for they were guarding the very message of God. Century by century they meticulously recorded every letter of Scripture onto the paper-like papyrus made of dried reeds, or onto the thin leather material called parchment. The original documents they relied on may have been lost, but some copies were amazingly preserved, thanks to the diligence of these devoted men and women.

When you review the facts, it's surprising that skeptics question the authenticity of the Bible. Scholars accept the writings of ancient individuals such as Aristotle or Virgil based on just a handful of documents. Yet by contrast, there are in many cases thousands of surviving copies of the texts that make up the Bible.

A famous example is the Dead Sea Scrolls. Shortly after World War II, shepherds and archaeologists discovered ancient jars in eleven caves near Qumran on the Dead Sea in the modern state of Israel. Hidden like time capsules for nearly two thousand years, the jars contained thousands of fragments representing between 825 and 870 writings. Portions of every book of the Old Testament except Esther were discovered. Some of these scrolls had circulated during the second century BC and the first century AD, making them centuries older than the best manuscripts scholars had available to them up to that time.

The Dead Sea Caves

A Reading from 2 Peter 1:20–21

You need to realize that no one alone can understand any of the prophecies in the Scriptures. The prophets did not think these things up on their own, but they were guided by the Spirit of God.

These significant translations and texts below are the primary sources of our modern versions of the Bible.

The Septuagint

The Old Testament was translated into Greek during the three centuries before Christ. "Septuagint" refers to the number 70; it was so named because it was believed that 72 Jewish scholars translated the Scriptures for the Egyptian Pharaoh Ptolemy II. The Septuagint is the canonical Old Testament of the Orthodox Church.

The Masoretic Text

Named for the Masoretes, the most influential group of Hebrew scribes, this text is the foundation for most modern translations of the Hebrew Bible. The oldest Masoretic manuscripts date from the 9th century AD.

The Aleppo Codex

Dated from the 10th century AD, this exquisite manuscript was possibly the first complete copy of the Masoretic Text. Written in Jerusalem and Tiberias, it was taken to Aleppo, Syria, in the 14th century, where it remained until it was returned, incomplete, to Israel in 1958.

The Vulgate

Saint Jerome's 4th century AD translation of the Bible into Latin remains a standard text in the Roman Catholic Church and is an important tool for helping scholars understand difficult passages in Hebrew and Greek texts.

Explosive Secret?

The Bible's message of love and freedom is both challenging and revolutionary, so much so that over the centuries wars have been fought because of it. Some early translators, who believed the Bible's message should be accessible to all, risked their reputations and even their lives to put it in the common tongue.

The thought of Bible translation as risky business can be difficult to understand today—not only are there hundreds of translations but hundreds of versions as well, including special editions designed for specific groups: sport coaches, business people, new brides, and retirees, to name only a few. There are even Bibles printed like magazines.

The first book that inventor Johannes Gutenberg produced on his revolutionary printing press in 1455 was the Bible. But its text was in Latin, and common people couldn't read it. At that time, governing rulers and religious authorities sought to keep a tight rein on Scripture, persecuting early translators like John Wycliffe (d. 1384) and William Tyndale (d. 1536), who believed that all Christians should have access to God's Word and be allowed to interpret it themselves.

Eventually, the King James Version, published in 1611, became the translation used by English-speaking Protestants. The Douay-Rheims predated the King James Version by a few years and was favored by Roman Catholics for the next four hundred years.

Johannes Gutenberg invented the printing press in the mid-15th century AD.

Woodcut of Gutenberg press in use
Jost Amman (1539–1591)

Deciding the Canon

Who decided what should be included in the Holy Bible—that is, what made it into "the canon"?

That's an important question, considering that hundreds of religious writings from antiquity—such as the *Gospel of Judas*—were not included. The answer, however, is not as mysterious as it might seem. For Christ and his followers, "the Scriptures" were the Torah and the Prophets, which had been written and used for centuries; hence Jesus' reference to the Law and the Prophets (see Luke 24:44). The list of books known as The Writings, the remaining books of the Hebrew Bible, was agreed upon during the second century AD, at which time the canon for the Old Testament was closed. For writings to be included in the New Testament, they had to be either written by an apostle or someone closely linked to the first generation of church leaders, and they had to be in continuous use by churches as well. The books that now make up the New Testament were already generally accepted when, in AD 367, church father Athanasius drew up his famous list of what we call the canon of Scripture.

Then why don't all Bibles have the same books? Roman Catholic and Orthodox Bibles include several Jewish writings that were preserved only in Greek rather than Hebrew versions. These include historical books like 1 & 2 Maccabees, dramatic stories like Tobit, Judith, and Susanna, and writings of great wisdom like Sirach.

Still, every Christian tradition regards books like the *Gospel of Judas* (which was widely publicized by the National Geographic Society after its publication in 2006) as "noncanonical"—that is, they do not belong in the Bible.

In the *Gospel of Judas*, a "good" Judas is depicted not as Christ's betrayer but as his liberator, commissioned to "sacrifice the man that clothes" Jesus. This is a classic view of the first- and second-century Gnostic sects that considered anything in the physical realm tainted. This set of beliefs was considered a heresy by the early church leaders who had known Jesus and those who were mentored by Jesus' disciples. Based on this, the Early Church intentionally omitted this book from the New Testament.

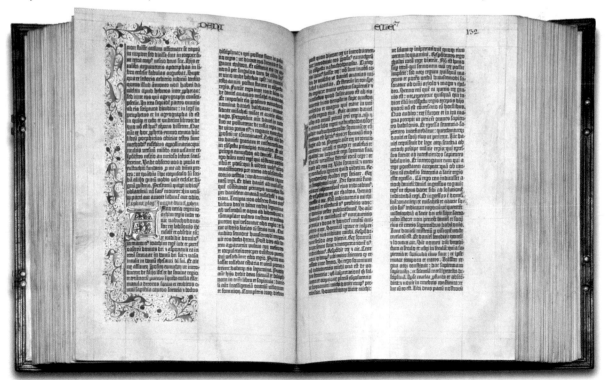

left: *St. Athanasius*
Mosaic. San Marco, Venice, Italy

Biblia Latina. Mainz, Germany (c. 1455)
Johannes Gutenberg (c. 1390/1400–1468) and Johann Fust (c. 1400–1466)

The Calling of the Apostles Peter and Andrew, 1308–11
Duccio Di Buoninsegna

CHAPTER 10

Ancient Prophecies Fulfilled:
Unveiling the Mysteries Surrounding the Son of God

From his provocative sermons to his astonishing miracles—turning water into wine, healing the sick, raising the dead, and more—the stories about Jesus surprise us. Who could have anticipated such a remarkable person?

As recorded by the New Testament writers, Jesus' actions were connected to the promises that God had made through ancient prophets about the one who would come in his name and champion his people. When Jesus' followers recalled the Hebrew Scriptures (the Old Testament), they saw countless signposts pointing to his life and ministry.

The prophet Jeremiah once spoke of a new agreement God would make with his people (31:31–34). Jesus claimed that his own shed blood and sacrificial death were the means by which that agreement was forged (Luke 22:20).

Not only was Jesus' life seen by many to fulfill prophecies, but Jesus was portrayed as a prophet in all four Gospels (Matthew 21:11, 46; Mark 6:15; Luke 7:16; 13:33; John 4:19; 6:14; 7:40; 9:17).

What prophetic mysteries became unraveled in the life and ministry of Jesus Christ?

God's Holy House:
A Sacred Space for All People

Jesus arrived in Jerusalem about a week before his death. He was traveling with his disciples to celebrate the Passover Festival, and as they approached the holy city, he told them to go to a nearby village and borrow a donkey for him to ride.

It may seem a ridiculous turn of events, but it was orchestrated to fulfill a key prophecy about the Messiah. Zechariah had anticipated a coming king who would enter Jerusalem in this very manner (9:9).

What happened next, according to Matthew, was just as remarkable: *"Jesus went into the temple and chased out everyone who was selling or buying"* (Matthew 21:12). What angered Jesus was probably not the buying and selling that was taking place. Often people traveled long distances and needed to change money and buy animals for their sacrifices once they arrived in Jerusalem. What aroused Jesus' anger was the dishonoring of the sacred place for worshiping God and the exploitation of the poor at the hands of these dishonest merchants.

The secret to Jesus' outburst can be found in an ancient piece of Scripture, which he quoted during his confrontation with the temple merchants: *"My house will be known as a house of worship for all nations"* (Isaiah 56:7).

Isaiah had predicted that God's temple would become a place for Jews and Gentiles to worship God. By reclaiming this sacred space for its intended purpose, Jesus connected his work to Isaiah's prophecy that all people would come to follow the God of Israel.

READ IT FOR YOURSELF

ISAIAH 56:6–7

Foreigners will follow me . . . I will bring them to my holy mountain, where they will celebrate in my house of worship. Their sacrifices and offerings will always be welcome on my altar. Then my house will be known as a house of worship for all nations.

HAGGAI

Jesus' passion in clearing the temple reminded his followers of the words of Haggai, an Old Testament prophet who preached during the time after the Israelites had returned to Jerusalem, following their long exile in Babylonia. At this low point of national and cultural pride, Haggai urged the Jews to rebuild Jerusalem's great temple, a symbol of unity and faith, as a sign that their nation was also finding the strength to rebuild itself.

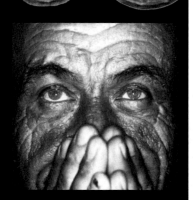

Jesus went into the temple and chased out everyone who was selling or buying. He turned over the tables of the moneychangers and the benches of the ones who were selling doves. He told them, "The Scriptures say, 'My house should be called a place of worship.' But you have turned it into a place where robbers hide." Blind and lame people came to Jesus in the temple, and he healed them. But the chief priests and the teachers of the Law of Moses were angry when they saw his miracles and heard the children shouting praises to the Son of David. The men said to Jesus, "Don't you hear what those children are saying?" "Yes, I do!" Jesus answered. "Don't you know that the Scriptures say, 'Children and infants will sing praises'?" Then Jesus left the city and went out to the village of Bethany, where he spent the night.

Matthew 21:12–17

The End of History:
One Secret Even Jesus Didn't Know

In addition to quoting Old Testament prophets, Jesus spoke a few prophecies of his own.

On more than one occasion he predicted his own death. He also spoke of a time when he would return to earth to inaugurate events associated with the final judgment and the coming of a new heaven and earth.

When pressed by his disciples, Jesus explained at length the events leading up to his second coming. But the precise timing, he insisted, was a mystery—even to himself. He claimed no one knew but God the Father when these events would take place (Matthew 24). While the book of Revelation, with its symbols and visions, is an apocalyptic book of the New Testament with close ties to the prophetic books in the Old Testament, Jesus' teachings included details about the mysterious events that would come to pass at the end of the present age.

READ IT FOR YOURSELF

MATTHEW 20:18–19

[Jesus said,] "The Son of Man will be handed over to the chief priests and the teachers of the Law of Moses. They will sentence him to death, and then they will hand him over to foreigners who will make fun of him. They will beat him and nail him to a cross. But on the third day he will rise from death."

Later, as Jesus was sitting on the Mount of Olives, his disciples came to him in private and asked, "When will this happen? What will be the sign of your coming and of the end of the world?"

Jesus answered:

"Don't let anyone fool you. Many will come and claim to be me. They will say they are the Messiah, and they will fool many people. You will soon hear about wars and threats of wars, but don't be afraid. These things will have to happen first, but that isn't the end. Nations and kingdoms will go to war against each other. People will starve to death, and in some places there will be earthquakes. But this is just the beginning of troubles.

"You will be arrested, punished, and even killed. Because of me, you will be hated by people of all nations. Many will give up and will betray and hate each other. Many false prophets will come and fool a lot of people. Evil will spread and cause many people to stop loving others. But if you keep on being faithful right to the end, you will be saved. When the good news about the kingdom has been preached all over the world and told to all nations, the end will come.

"Someday you will see that 'Horrible Thing' in the holy place, just as the prophet Daniel said. Everyone who reads this must try to understand! If you are living in Judea at that time, run to the mountains. If you are on the roof of your house, don't go inside to get anything. If you are out in the field, don't go back for your coat. It will be a terrible time for women who are expecting babies or nursing young children. And pray that you won't have to escape in winter or on a Sabbath. This will be the worst time of suffering since the beginning of the world, and nothing this terrible will ever happen again. If God doesn't make the time shorter, no one will be left alive. But because of God's chosen ones, he will make the time shorter.

"Someone may say, 'Here is the Messiah!' or 'There he is!' But don't believe it. False messiahs and false prophets will come and work great miracles and signs. They will even try to fool God's chosen ones. But I have warned you ahead of time. If you are told

the Messiah is out in the desert, don't go there! And if you are told he is in some secret place, don't believe it! The coming of the Son of Man will be like lightning that can be seen from east to west. Where there is a corpse, there will always be vultures.

"Right after those days of suffering, 'The sun will become dark, and the moon will no longer shine. The stars will fall, and the powers in the sky will be shaken.'

"Then a sign will appear in the sky. And there will be the Son of Man. All nations on earth will weep when they see the Son of Man coming on the clouds of heaven with power and great glory. At the sound of a loud trumpet, he will send his angels to bring his chosen ones together from all over the earth.

WHAT'S THE SIGN OF YOUR COMING?

"Learn a lesson from a fig tree. When its branches sprout and start putting out leaves, you know summer is near. So when you see all these things happening, you will know the time has almost come. I can promise you that some of the people of this generation will still be alive when all this happens. The sky and the earth won't last forever, but my words will.

"No one knows the day or hour. The angels in heaven don't know, and the Son himself doesn't know. Only the Father knows. When the Son of Man appears, things will be just as they were when Noah lived. People were eating, drinking, and getting married right up to the day the flood came and Noah went into the big boat. They didn't know anything was happening until the flood came and swept them all away. This is how it will be when the Son of Man appears. Two men will be in the same field, but only one will be taken. The other will be left. Two women will be together grinding grain, but only one will be taken. The other will be left. So be on your guard! You don't know when your Lord will come. Homeowners never know when a thief is coming, and they are always on guard to keep one from breaking in. Always be ready! You don't know when the Son of Man will come."

Matthew 24:3–44

Death and Life Foretold

Throughout Israel's history, the people of God looked forward to a deliverer—God's own champion who would come to their rescue. The prophecies regarding this champion described both a victorious king and a suffering servant. How one man could fill both roles was a secret that baffled even the greatest minds.

For those who believed Jesus to be the deliverer God had promised, they may have hoped that his life would reveal the more kingly elements of such a deliverer. Many would-be followers were understandably dismayed by his lifestyle and sacrificial death—both of which seemed unfitting of a mighty Messiah.

However, the key to unlocking the prophecies about Jesus is to understand them in terms of two advents (comings) described in Scripture—first, his birth, life and ministry, and subsequent sacrificial death, and then his coming again at the close of the age. The prophecies of a victorious, conquering king refer to the latter.

Overall, when Jesus first came, he did not raise a finger against Rome's military might. Instead, he urged his followers to turn the other cheek when attacked and walk the extra mile when necessary (Matthew 5:39). And in Jesus' final hours—in the very moment the long-awaited resistance could have begun at last—he told his followers to put away their swords and surrender to those who would put him to death (Matthew 26:52).

Unexpected Betrayal?

None of Jesus' disciples anticipated that Judas, one of their own, would double-cross Jesus for thirty pieces of silver. Yet even though Judas' betrayal carried the sting of surprise, several Old Testament prophecies pointed toward just such an unthinkable turn of events.

In anticipation of his disciple's treachery, Jesus quoted his ancestor King David lamenting the betrayal of a friend who once ate from the same table (see Psalm 41:9). Psalm 55:12–23 expresses similar heartbreak in response to a friend-turned-enemy—precisely what happened when Judas betrayed Jesus (John 13:21–26).

In the Jewish culture, sharing a meal carried special significance—and expectations—in terms of hospitality, loyalty, and even protection. According to the Gospel accounts, Judas shared the most important meal of Jesus' life—what is often referred to as the Last Supper—shortly before revealing Jesus' identity to his enemies. Thus, in betraying Jesus, he violated both his friend's trust and the customs of hospitality. And he did so for a bribe.

One of Zechariah's prophecies foreshadowed the sum Judas was paid for his betrayal—thirty pieces of silver (Zechariah 11:12–13; Matthew 26:15). Even in ancient times, this was not considered a significant amount. Zechariah underscored this fact, calling the payment "measly" and suggesting that it be thrown into the temple's treasury. According to Matthew, once Judas realized that Jesus was going to be put to death, he regretted what he had done and tried to return the money, throwing it into the treasury. But realizing it was too late to undo what he had done, Judas went out and hanged himself (Matthew 27:3–5). The book of Acts (1:18) reports that Judas died by throwing himself over a cliff.

A Surprising Silence

Ecce Homo, 1871
Antonio Ciseri (1821–1891)

READ IT FOR YOURSELF

MATTHEW 27:13–14

Pilate asked him, "Don't you hear what crimes they say you have done?" But Jesus did not say anything, and the governor was greatly amazed.

While the Servant Songs of Isaiah (42:1–4; 49:1–6; 50:4–9; 52:13–53:12) are often seen as pointing to God's people, the Israelites, Christian tradition also sees a hidden meaning in them, made clear only by the coming of Jesus—the one appointed to save God's people. So why did Isaiah picture a lamb being led to the slaughter? It just doesn't seem to fit the image of a mighty savior or king. For those closest to Jesus, this was one of the most heartbreaking mysteries of all, especially as Jesus stood silent before his accusers.

The Gospels recount the fulfillment of Isaiah's words, describing in detail how Jesus suffered abuse while neither protesting the accusations hurled his way nor even bothering to answer the charges against him (Matthew 27:11–14; Mark 15:2–5; Luke 23:3–5; John 18:33–38). When Pilate, the Roman governor, demanded that Jesus address the charges, Jesus responded as Isaiah said God's suffering servant would—with silence.

Some time after Jesus' death and resurrection, as the Christian Church was just emerging, a disciple named Philip encountered an Ethiopian official puzzling over the words of Isaiah's lyrical prophecy. Philip used the words of Isaiah to explain the hope of salvation available through Jesus, the Lamb of God who came to take away the sins of anyone who would believe in him. The ancient, mysterious prophecy became the catalyst by which the official heard and embraced the significance of Jesus' life and death (Acts 8:31–35).

Roman statue

***Christ before Pilate**, 1881*
Mihály Munkácsy (1844–1900)

A Reading from Acts 8:31–35

The official answered, "How can I understand unless someone helps me?" He then invited Philip to come up and sit beside him. The man was reading the passage that said, "He was led like a sheep on its way to be killed. He was silent as a lamb whose wool is being cut off, and he did not say a word. He was treated like a nobody and did not receive a fair trial. How can he have children, if his life is snatched away?" The official said to Philip, "Tell me, was the prophet talking about himself or about someone else?" So Philip began at this place in the Scriptures and explained the good news about Jesus.

Rejected King

Perhaps the cruelest irony of Jesus' death was that he became, in the words of the psalmist, "the stone that the builders tossed aside" (Psalm 118:22a). The New Testament quotes Psalm 118 no fewer than five times to highlight Jesus' painful rejection (Matthew 21:42; Mark 12:10; Luke 20:17; Acts 4:11; 1 Peter 2:7).

But the full quote reveals an even greater, more surprising irony: while rejected by those he came to save, Jesus was accepted by God. The secret of Jesus' suffering is that it was the means by which he became *"the most important stone"*—the cornerstone of God's spiritual house, the Church, which is made up of all of Jesus' followers (Psalm 118:22b; see also 1 Peter 2:4–7).

Jesus' suffering went beyond rejection; he was tortured and mocked as well. The Gospels describe how Jesus was spit on, blindfolded, and beaten (Matthew 26:67–68; Mark 14:65; Luke 22:63–65)—a tragic and brutal picture that several Old Testament passages anticipate. And quotes from the Psalms indicate that Jesus' followers looked beyond the traditional books of prophecy to find foreshadowings of Jesus as a suffering Messiah.

The Gospels describe in detail how these visions were fulfilled: the Roman soldiers guarding Jesus mocked him, clothing him in a scarlet robe (a sign of royalty), putting a twisted crown of thorns on his head, placing a wooden staff (a "reed") in his right hand, and sarcastically calling him the *"King of the Jews."* And just as the prophets foretold, they struck him in the face before leading him to his death (Isaiah 50:6; Micah 5:1; Matthew 27:27–30).